February, 2001

Dear Mr. Prager,
    I thoroughly enjoyed
your article in the "Journal"
of January, 31st.
    I hope that my book
proves to be of some interest
too.

            Best wishes

The Dodgers – Giants Rivalry 1900 - 1957

A Year by Year Retrospective

The Dodgers – Giants Rivalry 1900 - 1957

A Year by Year Retrospective

Marvin A. Cohen

Library of Congress Catalog Card Number: 00-132868

ISBN: 0-615-11154-8

First Printing   April 2000

Copies of this book are available from:

M C Productions
416 Main Street
Vestal, NY 13850

Author's eMail address: mcpro416@aol.com

Printed in the United State by
Morris Publishing
3212 East Highway 30
Kearney, NE 68847
1-800-650-7888

Dedication

To my wife, Cay, whose patience, support and computer wizardry made this book possible.

Acknowledgements

The author wishes to thank Dina Cohen for her tireless and insightful editing of the text. Any errors that remain are definitely my responsibility.

Thanks also go to Bill Burdick at the National Baseball Hall of Fame in Cooperstown, NY for his invaluable assistance in the selection of the photographs.

I would be remiss if I did not give credit to all of those who have amassed the statistics over the past century that are such an integral part of this book. Thanks to you all.

Table of Contents

Photographs

*Courtesy of the National Baseball Hall of Fame Library,
Cooperstown, NY*

Cover: Photograph of a Hy Sandham painting of a Boston – New
York game at the Polo Grounds in 1894.

Prologue

In 1939, the author, at the time a fatherless boy of seven, was taken to his first major league baseball game at storied Ebbets Field in Brooklyn. The two uncles, who had provided this rare treat at the peak of the Great Depression, had no idea as to the effect the midsummer double-header between the Cincinnati Reds and the Brooklyn Dodgers was having on the lad. The beautifully symmetrical field, the bright, green grass, the stunning white with blue trim uniforms of the home team, created an impression that is as vivid six decades later as it was on that day.

Growing up in Coney Island in the 1930's meant that even a seven-year old knew about baseball – the national pastime. In those days, the newspapers wrote about the game twelve months a year. Football, and its teams like the New York Giants, Brooklyn Dodgers, Chicago Bears, Washington Redskins, etc., were duly covered by the press during its brief season, but baseball was the game. All winter long, the daily articles in the newspapers, known as the "Hot Stove League," built up anticipation for the coming baseball season.

On the particular Sunday in question, Cincinnati, which had been a last-place team only two years before, but was now on its way to a pennant, used the Dodgers pitching staff for batting practice. Line drives were darting between the Brooklyn outfielders all afternoon, and a few found their way into the seats of the cozy ballpark.

The parade of Dodgers pitchers seemed endless, but the boy was particularly struck by one of them – an obviously overweight fellow in blue and white, with a glaringly protruding stomach, who was treated warmly by the Reds batters when he came in to relieve.

1

It was Freddie Fitzsimmons (actually, Frederick Landis Fitzsimmons), also known as "Fat Freddie," who, at age thirty-eight, definitely seemed to the boy to be past his prime. But baseball is an unpredictable game and "Fat Freddie" was to lead the Dodgers the following year with a superb 16-2 won-and-loss record.

Even two years later, in 1941, when the Dodgers electrified their long-suffering fans with a surprising pennant (their first in twenty-one years,) Freddie was still excelling with a 6-1 record until arm trouble effectively ended his career.

But of this, the boy knew nothing. The spectacle before him was opening up a new world of possibilities, one that was to provide a sort of background music for all of the events to follow in his life.

To that boy, and to the boy in all of us, this book is dedicated.

The Early Years – The Rivalry Begins

The Brooklyn Dodgers and the New York Giants. Merely mentioning this rivalry can still stir the emotions of those who fanatically rooted for their heroes "when it was a game." For those of us who grew up in New York City when it had three teams, these two National League rivals filled our often uneventful lives with a much needed passion and distraction. When "our" team won, life was good – when they lost, we felt real despair.

Their twenty-two meetings each season were more than just regularly scheduled baseball games – they were events. We knew the players, their nicknames, their strong and weak points and we loved them as if they were family – that is, if they played for "our" team. When they were traded, as they sometimes were, from one to the other, they became instant enemies.

What we considered "real" fans rooted for either the Dodgers or the Giants. Yankees fans were treated with utter disdain. Anyone could root for a consistent winner. The Dodgers and Giants needed our support and our affection and we gave them freely.

No other city had three teams, although there were others that had two: notably, Boston with the Red Sox and Braves (Bees, for a time); St. Louis, with the Cardinals and Browns; Philadelphia, with the Phillies and Athletics and, of course, Chicago, which can still boast of having the Cubs and the White Sox. However, all of these cities had the sensible arrangement of having one team in each of the two major leagues. Only in New York, did two National League teams (out of a total of eight) meet head-on for twenty-two of their 154 games.

The reasons for this unique arrangement go back to the origins of organized baseball itself. After decades of amateur baseball, and a plethora of teams, a convention of representatives from twenty-five different clubs met on March 10, 1858 to form the first baseball league. Called the National Association of Base Ball Players, it still consisted of amateurs playing for side bets and/or prestige and bragging rights. Even here, at the very dawning of modern baseball, the natural rivalry between the Brooklyn and New York teams was recognized. A series of "all-star" games between the teams from the two cities was organized (Brooklyn was a city until 1898) and, on July 20th of that year, a date cherished by all future club owners, the first admission (50 cents) was charged to see a game. On that date, 1,500 fans saw New York beat Brooklyn by a score of 22-18.

The Excelsiors of Brooklyn were the first organized baseball club to go on tour. Their convincing victories over teams from New York State, Philadelphia and Baltimore attracted attention for baseball nationwide through newspaper reports of their prowess. Even Walt Whitman, writing after an Excelsior loss, (when he was editor of the "Brooklyn Daily Eagle") exulted that the Excelsiors have "always reflected credit upon the manly and healthful game they practice." The Atlantic Club of Brooklyn later was the champion of the 28 teams in the area in 1861, 1864 and 1865, while the rival New York Eckfords won the title in 1862 and were unbeaten in 1863. (Not everyone was in the Union army during the Civil War.)

Unfortunately, the heavy betting associated with all of these "amateur" games often led to bribes and the throwing of the contests. Also, by the late 1860's, star players were being paid – either with jobs or money "under the table." Finally, in answer to all of the chicanery, the legendary Cincinnati Red Stockings were formed as a professional team in 1869. They played every important amateur club from coast to coast and beat them all. Actually, they won ninety-two consecutive games before the Atlantics of Brooklyn beat them in eleven innings, on June 14,

1870. (Prior to that date, games ended in ties. This was the first recorded game to go into extra innings.)

The success of the Red Stockings proved conclusively that amateurs could not compete with professionals and spurred other cities to seek the acclaim that Cincinnati had attained with their club. (Certainly, it was not financial success that caught everyone's attention. In their first year of operation, the Red Stockings showed a net profit of exactly $1.39! Proceeds were $29,726.26, while salaries and expenses totaled $29,724.87.)

The National Association of Professional Base-Ball Players was formed in 1871. In a display of tight-fistedness that foreshadowed Branch Rickey's arrival, Brooklyn disdained risking the $10 fee required to join. However, the New York Mutuals, owned by no less a personage than Boss Tweed himself, were represented. To no one's surprise, gambling destroyed this association too. A wave of reform followed and led to the formation of the National League in 1876.

New York was a charter member, playing a full seventy-game schedule to start the season. These games were all against the visiting western teams. The Giants could be tight-fisted too; so when they joined with Philadelphia in refusing to honor their commitments by risking the expense of going out west to play the teams that had already come east, they were expelled in mid-season.

By 1883, cooler heads had prevailed. New York was back in the National League for good. Brooklyn, which had thrown in its lot with the rival, American Association, fielded teams in both leagues in 1890. They stunned everyone by winning the National League pennant in their first try. They gave up their American Association membership after this season – perhaps influenced by their last-place finish in that organization. In any case, by 1890, the historic rivalry between Brooklyn and the New York Giants had officially begun.

It would continue unabated for sixty-seven years when, suddenly, both franchises disappeared in a cloud of greed from the New York City scene.

Like life itself, baseball is a game of cycles. Teams that are dynasties in one decade can find themselves to be also-rans in the next. Sometimes it is management that creates powerhouses by spending a great deal of money. The Yankees did just that when they acquired Babe Ruth from a cash strapped Boston Red Sox organization. Management can destroy a championship team as well – witness the dismantling of the Philadelphia Athletics in 1915 and the Florida Marlins in 1998.

However, money alone is not always enough to ensure a team's fortune. High-priced regulars can falter or suffer injuries, or another team's rookies can begin their careers in a blaze of glory and carry a team to an unexpected pennant. Reese and Reiser did that for the Dodgers in 1941, Mays did it for the Giants in 1951 and the "Whiz Kids" of Philadelphia did it in 1950, as just a few examples of surprise pennant winners.

The cycles come and go and often the game itself changes with them, thus making it even more difficult to evaluate the performances of teams like the Dodgers and the Giants. Let us recall that there was a "dead ball" era in the game and, mainly due to the attention drawn to the game by Babe Ruth's home runs, a "lively ball" era began. Two world wars and a major depression have also intervened during the period of our interest to further complicate any attempts at comparison.

Shall the argument be settled by simply counting the pennants won from 1900-1957? (In 1958, the Giants and Dodgers deserted their roots and moved to the West Coast.) Using that criterion, the Giants would win hands-down. From 1900 to 1957 the Giants won fifteen pennants, the Dodgers won only ten. On the other hand, the Giants were last five times during that period, the Dodgers only once.

6

To make the apparent superiority of the Giants even more convincing, let it be noted that during those years, the Giants won 361 more games, hit an astounding 1,147 more home runs and had 1,794 more RBI's than the Dodgers. Statistics don't lie, do they? Well, they can if we look only at selected ones. What we will attempt to do is to look at the two clubs overall performance, on a year-by-year basis, not just their league standings. This entails taking into consideration: batting, pitching, individual honors and any intangibles that we can throw into the mix.

We obviously cannot measure who was more fiery – John McGraw or Leo Durocher, but we can look at the results of their efforts. We can consider questions such as: can a Duke Snider be compared to the Giants legend, Mel Ott or how does the Dodgers pitching ace, Dazzy Vance stack up against the Giants Christy Mathewson? The answers may surprise you.

Join me now as we take a year-by-year look at two of the greatest sports franchises of the twentieth century. How did they fare against each other and the rest of the league? Who were the personalities that fueled the competition? Who was better? Read on – then you decide.

NOTE: The Brooklyn team, variously called: Excelsiors, the Atlantic Club, the Bridegrooms, the Trolley Dodgers, Superbas, the Flock, and even the Robins (after Wilbert Robinson became manager in 1914) will be called Dodgers throughout this book to avoid unnecessary confusion.

Where the rivalry began – 19th Century Action: Polo Grounds *(above);* Washington Park *(below).*

1900

Brooklyn Triumphs

As the twentieth century dawned in 1900, Brooklyn fans were treated to their team's winning of a second consecutive pennant. To make the victory even sweeter, their hated cross-town rivals, the New York Giants, finished last for the first time in their history.

The two first-place finishes in 1899 and 1900 were quite a turnaround for the Brooklyn Club. Things had been so bad in 1898 that Charlie Ebbets, who had gone from selling peanuts in the stands to team president, had made himself the third manager that year. He "led" the team to a 38-68 won-lost record and a dismal tenth-place finish in a then twelve team league.

Ebbets, who would remain the club's president until 1925, had the good sense and humility at the end of 1898 to bring over Ned Hanlon, formerly of the Baltimore Orioles, to become manager. Hanlon, in turn, had enough foresight to bring with him Wee Willie Keeler, already a two-time batting champion, and others. After winning the pennant for Brooklyn in 1899, Hanlon then enticed Iron Man McGinnity over from the Orioles. All McGinnity did was to win twenty-nine games to lead the league in 1900.

In addition to winning twenty-nine games and losing only nine, McGinnity earned his "Iron Man" nickname by tying Bill Carrick of the Giants for most games started (45) and leading the league in innings pitched with 347. Considering that McGinnity was already twenty-eight when he pitched his first major league game, he managed, in a ten year career (six of them with the Giants,) to pitch more than 3,450 innings and to appear in 466 games.

The Superbas, as the Brooklyn team was then known, scored 816 runs – an amazing total in the dead ball era, and not to be duplicated for a dozen years, when a cork-centered ball began to be used. Led by Keeler's .368 batting average, they topped the league in hitting with a .293 average. The entire team struck out only 272 times. Keeler also achieved his seventh consecutive 200-hit season in 1900. (He punched out 204 hits in just 136 games.) Joe Kelley, who Hanlon had brought over from Baltimore in 1899, where he hit .330, "slipped" to .319 in 1900, but did lead the club in RBI's with ninety-one and in home runs with six!

Even with all of his available talent, Hanlon had to struggle to beat out a Pittsburgh team that featured Honus Wagner. Wagner led the league in hitting with a .381 average. Pittsburgh also had Rube Waddell. The mound ace was in the process of winning the first of his seven league-leading titles for strikeouts with 130, and, in addition, posting the National League's best earned run average, a nifty 2.37. Waddell eventually retired with the sixth-best ERA in baseball history – 2.16.

Meanwhile, the last-place Giants offered a first baseman, Jack Doyle, who set a modern day record of errors for a first baseman with forty-three. In fact, the entire team's fielding record was a poor .928. Their third baseman, "Piano Legs" Hickman, led the league with eighty-six errors; the most for any player at any position. He somewhat redeemed himself by leading the club in RBI's with 91.

The Giants best pitcher, Bill Carrick, won nineteen games, but he also lost a league-leading twenty-two. He finished thirty-two of the games that he started and had a respectable ERA of 3.53. Known as "Doughnut Bill" (because he liked them, not because he threw a "sinker"), his career lasted for only five years. Sharing ERA honors with Carrick for the Giants was Pink Hawley. In this, the only year that he pitched for the Giants, Hawley also led them in strikeouts with eighty.

Fortunately for the Giants, their fortunes were about to change dramatically. In midseason, Cincinnati traded a youngster to them named Christy Mathewson. In his first full campaign, a year later, Mathewson would win twenty games and pitch a no-hitter.

Dodgers		1900	Giants	
Willie Keeler	.368	**BA**	Kip Selbach	.337
Joe Kelley	91	**RBI**	"Piano Legs" Hickman	91
" "	6	**HR**	" " " " Charles Taylor	9
Joe McGinnity	29*	**WINS**	Bill Carrick	19
" "	2.90	**ERA**	" " " Pink Hawley	3.53
" "	93	**SO**	" " "	80

* led the National League

11

1901

A.L. Upstarts Create Havoc

Many expected Hanlon and his Brooklyn squad to repeat their success in 1901 for a third straight year, but this was not to be. In fact, Hanlon never won another pennant with any team. In 1901, the upstart American League had begun its first year of existence, despite the sneers of the established National League, which was preparing for its twenty-fifth season. The sneers would soon turn to annoyance and then outrage.

With the American League desperate for players to establish its credibility, a bidding war erupted and, for the first time, players suddenly had a choice of clubs to play with that were willing to pay them a decent salary. Teams like Brooklyn, which lost Iron Man McGinnity, suffered. The Pirates, on the other hand, lost very little and therefore coasted to the pennant – seven games ahead of Philadelphia and eleven games ahead of defending champion Brooklyn.

Although the Giants moved up a notch to seventh place, they had little but Mathewson to brag about. Actually, Brooklyn even had bragging rights in the pitching department, as their own "Wild Bill" Donovan, out of Laurence, Massachusetts, led the National League with twenty-five wins. Brooklyn's team batting average, with such worthies as Keeler and Sheckard averaging over .350, topped the Giants team batting percentage by twenty-four points. Their team slugging average was sixty-nine points higher than the Giants and they had more hits (164) and thirteen more home runs. Brooklyn had thirty-two round trippers to New York's nineteen.

Keeler's ability to foul off pitches led directly to a new rule being instituted in both leagues in 1903. For the first time, foul balls were to be considered strikes – except, of course, for strike three. Wee Willie hit .355 for the year and Sheckard led the club with 104 RBI's and eleven home runs.

Sheckard also set a National League record that still stands, when he hit a grand slam homer in two consecutive games on September 23rd and 24th. While no other National League hitter has ever matched this feat, five American Leaguers, including, of course, Babe Ruth, have.

In the pitching department for Brooklyn, besides winning twenty-five games, Donovan was the team leader in ERA and strikeouts. He managed to strike out five more than Mathewson, who had a great year for the Giants.

Mathewson led the Giants in wins, with twenty. He also led in ERA (2.41) and strikeouts (221). In addition, he pitched the first no-hit game of the new century for the Giants against St. Louis, beating them 5-0 on July 15th. Dummy Taylor was the workhorse of the Giants staff. He led the National League in games started (45) and complete games (43). He also topped the league in hits allowed (377).

The Giants had little else to crow about. While their best hitter, George Van Haltren, did hit a nifty .342, their best RBI man, John Ganzel, was far behind Sheckard with only sixty-six. George Davis, who led the club with seven homers, hit .309. He and Van Haltren were the Giants only .300 hitters. While Ganzel did lead a weak hitting club in RBI's, he hit only .215 in 138 games. The team had only nineteen homers. Only Chicago had less with eighteen round-trippers. Unfortunately for their fans, the Giants would be even worse in 1902.

13

Dodgers		1901	Giants	
Willie Keeler	.355	**BA**	George Van Haltren	.342
Jimmy Sheckard	104	**RBI**	John Ganzel	66
" "	11	**HR**	George Davis	7
Wild Bill Donovan	25*	**WINS**	Christy Mathewson	20
" " "	2.77	**ERA**	" " "	2.41
" " "	226	**SO**	" " "	221

* led the National League

1902

John McGraw Arrives in New York

In 1902, Brooklyn climbed back up to second place, but still finished a full twenty-eight games behind an electrifying Pittsburgh club that won 103 games, while losing only thirty-six. Pittsburgh had once again avoided the depredations of the rival American League, while the hapless also-rans in the National League continued to lose their stars. Good pitching (all five Brooklyn starters had ERA's under 3.00) and a .338 batting average by Keeler allowed the Dodgers to finish second. Unfortunately, Keeler was the only .300 hitter on the team. Bill Dahlen led the club in RBI's with seventy-four.

This was Keeler's last hurrah in a Brooklyn uniform. More raids in 1903 by the American League cost the Dodgers Keeler, their best pitcher, Wild Bill Donovan, and their nineteen game winner, Frank Kitson. It would take Brooklyn twelve agonizing years of second division finishes to recover.

The Giants had a new manager, out of Truxton, NY, named John McGraw, for the last sixty-three games of the season, and new stars like McGinnity, who had returned to the National League. Roger Bresnehan and Dan McGann were also added to the club. Unfortunately, a terrible start preceded McGraw's arrival, and they ended the season dead last again. Mathewson led the staff with only fourteen wins, while McGinnity produced a sparkling 2.06 ERA for a rare highlight. Mathewson also led the club with 159 strikeouts. Their offense is best exemplified by the fact that Billy Lauder topped the club with only forty-four RBI's.

Concerning the Giants new manager, the following anecdote can possibly tell volumes about the man. While a player for the Baltimore Orioles, his feuding with the President of the American League, Ban Johnson, had already reached epic proportions – mainly due to McGraw's violent behavior on the field. McGraw, already known as the undisputed king of the umpire baiters, had been suspended once by Johnson for verbal abuse. (In this era, when umpire-baiting was a common practice, it took an unusual performance to warrant a suspension.) McGraw, however, felt that he was unjustly becoming a marked man. His fears may have been proven justified when, in April of 1902, he was hit five times in the same game and was never awarded first base! (The umpire, Jack Sheridan, claimed that McGraw was allowing himself to be hit intentionally and was, therefore, not entitled to first base.) To add insult to the five injuries that McGraw incurred, he was ejected from the game for arguing Sheridan's interpretation of the rules and was subsequently suspended by the league office for five days. (Perhaps a day for each time that he was hit by a pitch?)

McGraw got his revenge against Johnson and the American League. He convinced two National League owners to buy the Oriole's stock, release almost the entire lineup to the Giants and Reds and then get himself named the new manager of the Giants!

Fireworks were sure to follow and they did. The American League, led by an angry Ban Johnson himself, took over the Baltimore franchise that McGraw had just decimated and, a year later, moved it to New York to compete with McGraw's Giants. So, one can argue that the new club, the Highlanders, later, the New York Yankees, were born out of the spiteful revenge of John McGraw and of Ban Johnson. A surprisingly tainted beginning for what was to become such a storied franchise.

However, as is so often the case, fate had the last laugh on John McGraw. Although he has gone down in history as the second winningest manager in the game – Connie Mack is first – he holds the record for losing the most World Series games to the league that he felt had harassed him. (His record might have been even worse, if he had not refused to meet the American League champions in 1904.)

Brooklyn won seventy-five games in 1902, the Giants only forty-eight. The Giants hit only eight home runs all season, while Brooklyn clouted nineteen. That was a fair amount for a club in this dead ball era and was actually enough to give Brooklyn a tie with Pittsburgh for the league lead in that department. Their Tommy Leach, had six of those homers to lead the league in that department. It stands as the lowest total to win that honor in the twentieth century.

The contentious Andrew Freedman stepped down as president of the Giants at the end of the year. After a number of refusals, Freedman had reluctantly brought in the right man, John McGraw, to lead the club. Unfortunately for Freedman, he would not be there to share in the glory years to follow.

Dodgers		1902	Giants	
Willie Keeler	.338*	**BA**	Dan McGann	.301
Bill Dahlen	74	**RBI**	Billy Lauder	44
Tom McCreery Jimmy Sheckard	4	**HR**	Steve Brodie	3
Frank Kitson	19	**WINS**	Christy Mathewson	14
Doc Newton	2.42	**ERA**	Joe McGinnity	2.06
Wild Bill Donovan	170	**SO**	Christy Mathewson	159

* led the National League

1903

The Year of Mathewson and McGinnity

In 1903, Brooklyn slumped to fifth place as the Pirates won their third consecutive pennant. Legendary Honus Wagner, finally elevated from utility man to permanent shortstop, led the charge. Once installed at shortstop, Wagner retained the position for the rest of his long career.

The Giants not only had their pugnacious leader, John McGraw, for the entire season, but they were able to boast two thirty-game winners: Christy Mathewson and Joe "Iron Man" McGinnity (the ex-Oriole and Brooklyn Dodger). The Iron Man lived up to his name by starting forty-eight games, a major league record that still stands, and completing all but four of them! He also set a National League record by pitching an astounding total of 434 innings.

On the strength of their aces' pitching heroics, the Giants moved from last place in 1902, to second place in 1903. Their pitchers led the league in strikeouts with 628. Mathewson had 267 of these to lead the league.

It was an auspicious beginning both for McGraw and the new president of the Giants, John T. Brush. It helped that Roger Bresnehan hit .350, to lead the club, and that Sam Mertes led the league in RBI's with 104.

By comparison, the fifth-place Brooklyn pitching staff posted 438 strikeouts and, even the pennant-winning Pirates had only 454. Ned Garvin led the Dodgers with 154, but Henry Schmidt proved to be the ace of the staff with twenty-two wins and only thirteen losses.

Major League baseball was not a desirable career for everyone in those days, both in regard to salaries and personal reputation. Despite the great year, Schmidt left baseball for good at the end of the season.

Brooklyn could also boast that they had the league's leading home run hitter. Jimmy Sheckard hit nine to take that title. (The entire, last-place, St. Louis team hit only eight!) The dead ball era was obviously in full swing.

Sheckard also topped the Dodgers in batting, with a .332 average, and led the National League in stolen bases with sixty-seven. At the tender age of twenty-four, the left-handed hitting outfielder could clearly do it all. The Dodgers would not see his like again until the appearance of Pete Reiser in 1940.

Despite their amazing season and Honus Wagner, the Pirates lost to the Boston club of the rival American League in the first ever World Series by five games to three. On a final note to the 1903 season, baseball proved that it was not only a dangerous game for the players – what with flying spikes and bean balls being thrown regularly at batters without helmets – but for the fans too. In Philadelphia, the Phillies watched in horror as part of their park, the Baker Bowl, collapsed during a game. Twelve spectators were killed.

Dodgers		1903	Giants	
Jimmy Sheckard	.332	**BA**	Roger Bresnehan	.350
Jack Doyle	91	**RBI**	Sam Mertes	104*
Jimmy Sheckard	9*	**HR**	" "	7
Henry Schmidt	22	**WINS**	Joe McGinnity	31*
Oscar Jones	2.94	**ERA**	Christy Mathewson	2.26
Ned Garvin	154	**SO**	" "	267*

* led the National League

19

1904

Giants Snub the A.L.

1904 was the first year of a uniform, 154-game schedule in both leagues. The Giants met this challenge with a roster of seventeen players!

Pitching was the difference again, despite the expanded schedule. The Giants staff had an ERA that was an astounding fifty-three points lower than that of the Brooklyn pitchers. They also gave up sixty-five fewer walks and struck out 254 more batters. To make matters worse, Brooklyn's pitchers gave up 130 more hits than did their Giants counterparts.

Even for the "Dead ball" era, the Brooklyn team batting average was dismal (.232). The Giants were thirty points higher and scored two hundred more runs.

The New York club, despite the lack of a .300 hitter, led the league in a number of areas: BA - .262; FA - .956; Runs – 744; Home runs – 31; Steals – 283 and ERA – 2.17. This constituted almost a clean sweep of league honors. The only bright spot for Brooklyn was that their slugger, Harry Lumley, led the league in home runs by belting nine. He also led the National League in triples with eighteen.

The Giants set a Major League record with 106 wins, much of their success coming against the weaker clubs in the Eastern division. Against Brooklyn, Boston and Philadelphia, the Giants had a record of fifty-six wins and only nine losses! They won in bunches. At one point, in midsummer, they won eighteen in a row and finished the season with fifty-three wins in their last seventy-one games.

This was McGraw's first pennant winner as a manager. However, it did not sweeten his on-field personality. He warmed up for the season by baiting an umpire so badly during spring training that his impressionable players beat the poor soul unconscious after the game. McGraw exhibited even less class at the end of the season when, supported by team president, John T. Brush, he refused to play in a World Series with the champions of that "minor league," the Boston Red Sox. The owners got together that winter to make sure that this could never happen again. The guidelines that they created for an annual World Series are pretty much followed today.

The Giants pitching tandem of McGinnity and Mathewson were once again outstanding. Between them, they set a modern record for two pitchers on the same team by recording sixty-eight wins between them. Mathewson also led the league in strikeouts with 212. No other National League pitcher struck out as many as 200.

In a year when Jim O'Rourke caught a full game for the Giants at age fifty-two, a well-traveled infielder, Herman Long, retired at the end of the season, at the tender age of thirty-eight. Long will be remembered by trivia fans as the only major leaguer to compile 1,000 or more errors over a career. Sadly, by 1909 he was dead.

Although the Giants statistical advantage in 1904 appears to be overwhelming, Brooklyn's individual batting totals were surprisingly competitive. Doc Gessler led Brooklyn with a .290 batting average, surpassing the Giants leader, Dan McGann, who hit .286. (McGann could run too; he set a National League record by stealing five bases in one game.) The Giants Bill Dahlen, traded to the Giants by Brooklyn the previous winter, led the league with eighty RBI's, but Brooklyn's Harry Lumley was right behind him with seventy-eight. Even in the pitching department, while

McGinnity led the league in ERA with a 1.61, Brooklyn's Ned Garvin had a very respectable 1.68. Of course, McGinnity's thirty-five wins were more than double the Dodgers leader, Oscar Jones, who won seventeen and Mathewson had 102 more strikeouts than Brooklyn's leader, Jack Cronin, who had 110.

Dodgers		1904	Giants	
Doc Gessler	.290	**BA**	Dan McGann	.286
Harry Lumley	78	**RBI**	Bill Dahlen	80*
" "	9*	**HR**	Dan McGann	6
Oscar Jones	17	**WINS**	Joe McGinnity	35*
Ned Garvin	1.68	**ERA**	" "	1.61*
Jack Cronin	110	**SO**	Christy Mathewson	212*

* led the National League

1905

The Giants Are World Champions

1905 brought the Giants even greater glory. Christy Mathewson won thirty or more games for the third consecutive year. He also led the National League in ERA (1.27) and shutouts, with eight. To top things off, he became the first pitcher in the twentieth century to pitch two no-hitters. With Mike Donlin batting a league-leading .356, in a year when only three batters in the entire American League reached .300, the Giants took over first place on April 23rd and were never seriously challenged.

This was also the year that their third baseman, Art Devlin, stole fifty-nine bases. No Major League third baseman has ever stolen more.

McGraw's managerial genius was much in evidence in his use of switch hitter Sammy Strang. (He was acquired from Brooklyn.) McGraw sent Sammy to the plate fourteen times in a "pinch," which led baseball writers to coin the term: "pinch-hitter." Strang's real name was Sammy Strang Nicklin, but he dropped the "Nicklin" because his father – despite being the owner of the Nashville team in the Southern League – objected to his son playing professional baseball. One can only imagine Sammy's father's feelings about the next step in his son's career, when Sammy began studying with a voice teacher so that he could pursue stardom on the musical stage!

The Giants proved their mettle in the World Series too. Their pitching staff, behind the amazing Mathewson's three shutouts, allowed them to sweep past the stunned Athletics of Philadelphia. The Giants ERA for the World Series was a perfect 0.00.

After such a year, most pundits were predicting a dynasty for the Giants, but it was not to be. Who would have guessed that they would have to wait six long years for their next pennant?

As for McGraw, himself, despite all the success, he was still unable to control his temper. He was suspended for fifteen days and fined $1,540 (a not insignificant sum in those days) for his continued umpire baiting. Considering the general umpire baiting that was part of the game at the time, McGraw had to be in consistently rare form to attract this kind of attention.

Meanwhile, the hapless Brooklyn Club sank to last place. It was the first and, surprisingly, would be the last time that they would ever be cellar dwellers in their Brooklyn uniforms. Everything seemed to go wrong. In a year when the dead ball was king, the Dodgers had a pitching staff that managed to compile an ERA of 3.76. (The Giants staff, by comparison, posted a 2.39.) Brooklyn's pitchers gave up more than a hit per inning pitched, walked 112 more batters than did the Giants and struck out 204 less.

None of Brooklyn's hitters reached .300 and Heinie Batch actually led the club with only forty-nine RBI's. Even the individual home run title eluded them as Lumley dropped to seven round-trippers for the year. To rub salt into that particular wound, the home run leader for 1905 in the National League was one Fred Odwell of Cincinnati. Odwell hit nine. The irony was that Odwell had hit only one home run the previous year, and never hit another in the Major Leagues.

Dodgers		1905	Giants	
Harry Lumley	.293	**BA**	Mike Donlin	.356
Heinie Batch	49	**RBI**	Sam Mertes	108
Harry Lumley	7	**HR**	Bill Dahlen Mike Donlin	7
Doc Scanlan	15	**WINS**	Christy Mathewson	32*
" "	2.92	**ERA**	" " "	1.27*
Harry McIntire Doc Scanlan	135	**SO**	" " "	206*

* led the National League

1906

Brooklyn Continues to Slumber

Brooklyn continued to languish in the second division in 1906, although they did manage to rise from last to fifth place. This was mainly due to an improved pitching staff that lowered its ERA from 3.76 the previous year to 3.13. Whereas, in 1905 only Doc Scanlan, out of Syracuse, New York, won more than eight games (he won fifteen), in 1906 Stricklett, McIntire and Eason joined him as double digit winners. Scanlon was the leader once again, this time with eighteen victories, and rookie Jim Pastorius chipped in with ten wins. Unfortunately, of the five hurlers who won ten or more games, only Scanlan won more than he lost.

McIntire, who had broken in with a disheartening total of twenty-five losses, as against only eight wins the previous year, posted a more respectable thirteen and twenty-one record. He also led the staff in strikeouts with 121, beating Scanlan by one. McIntire's high point of the season was a ten-inning no-hitter that he threw on August 1st. Unfortunately, Brooklyn, which had already been no-hit by the Phillies Johnny Lush, in April, could not score either and McIntire lost his no-hitter in the eleventh inning.

Mal Eason gained some retribution for Brooklyn by no-hitting St. Louis on July 20th. It was a rare highlight in an undistinguished season for the struggling club as it posted its first no-hit game in the twentieth century. Coincidentally, both the Giants and the Dodgers achieved their first no-hit games of the new century against the Cardinals.

The individual home run leader in the National League was, once again, a Dodger, as Tim Jordan slammed twelve to take the honor. His closest competitor was teammate Harry Lumley with nine. (Lumley's .477 slugging average also led the National League.) Thanks to these two, Brooklyn led the league in home runs with twenty-five!

The favored Giants were surprised by Frank Chance and his Chicago Cubs, who ran away with the pennant by a twenty-game margin. The Giants might have seen the handwriting on the wall on June 7th, when their ace, Christy Mathewson, was blasted for six runs in a third of an inning by the Cubs on their way to a 19-0 rout.

Chance had taken over as player-manager midway through the previous season and, in his first full year at the helm, led the Cubs to a remarkable 116-36 record. Like McGraw, Chance was a well-respected umpire-baiter, but for this season he was able to sit calmly by as his club racked up victory after victory. McGraw, on the other hand, marred his record once more by engaging in a vicious fight with a Phillies rookie infielder named Paul Sentell that made headlines.

Most fans are aware of McGraw's managerial accomplishments, and quick temper, but many are unaware of what a talented player he was. He was as ferocious a competitor on the field, as he was off the bench. The game itself was more of a war when he played, with beanballs and spikings the norm. In any case, by the time that he finished his playing career, hobbled by injuries, he had accumulated a lifetime batting average of .334 and even had thirteen home runs in the dead ball era. McGraw had talent – he could compete with Keeler in his ability to foul balls off until he got one he liked, and his prowess at this art heavily influenced the decision by Major League baseball to call the first two foul balls strikes. Spending most of his career as a left-handed hitting shortstop and third baseman, McGraw was a star performer for an eleven-year period from 1891 – 1901 before injuries slowed him down.

McGinnity and Mathewson once again won more than twenty games each for the Giants. At age thirty-five, McGinnity led the league with twenty-seven wins. Luther (Dummy) Taylor, who received his "kind" nickname by virtue of the fact that he was totally deaf, had lost twenty-seven games for the Giants in 1902 and had been briefly exiled to Cleveland of the American League. Gratefully returning to the Giants, Taylor had a stellar year. The Oskaloosa, Kansas native led the club in ERA with a 2.20 and won seventeen games.

The Giants led the league in stolen bases and had three .300 hitters, but it was not nearly enough to overtake Tinker to Evers to Chance. An interesting sidelight to the Giants season was the only Major League pitching start by Christy Mathewson's brother, Henry. No "chip off the old block," Henry walked a record fourteen batters and disappeared from the big show permanently.

Dodgers		1906	Giants	
Harry Lumley	.324	**BA**	Cy Seymour	.320
Tim Jordan	78	**RBI**	Art Devlin	65
" "	12*	**HR**	Cy Seymour Sammy Strang	4
Doc Scanlan	18	**WINS**	Joe McGinnity	27*
Elmer Stricklett	2.71	**ERA**	Dummy Taylor	2.20
Harry McIntire	121	**SO**	Red Ames	156

* led the National League

1907

Mathewson Continues to Sparkle

The Chicago Cubs, who had amazed the baseball world in 1906 by winning 116 games, "slumped" to a 107-45 record in 1907. It was still enough to easily repeat as National League champions. All five of Chicago's starting pitchers had ERA's under 2.00! The total staff ERA was an amazing 1.73. By comparison, the second place Pirates were next best with an ERA of 2.30.

The Giants actually led Chicago by three games late in August, despite low morale due to pay cuts by management. (Mike Donlin, a .300 hitter in 1906, before breaking his leg, sat out the entire season in protest.)

The Cubs took three of a four-game series at home on the last four days of August, behind Jack, "the Giant Killer," Pfiester, who won two of them, and never looked back. McGraw had done a masterful job of managing, but the Cubs were too talented to be denied.

The Brooklyn club finished fifth in 1907, while the Giants made it to the first division with a fourth place finish. Their team performances, however, were not consistent with their proximity in the league standings.

The Giants won seventeen more games (82-65) and scored 127 more runs than did Brooklyn. Their team batting average was nineteen points higher and, although neither team could boast a .300 hitter, the Giants did lead the National League in home runs with twenty-three. Cy Seymour was the leading Giants hitter, with a .294 batting average; Tim Jordan led Brooklyn with a .274.

Giants outfielder Spike Shannon led the league in at-bats (585) and runs scored (104). Whitey Alperman, a speedy Brooklyn utility infielder was tops in triples for the National League, with sixteen.

Giants pitchers walked ninety-four fewer batters than did the Brooklyn staff and struck out 176 more. On an individual basis, the great Christy Mathewson of the Giants led the league in wins with twenty-four and strikeouts, 178. He led the club in ERA too, with a sparkling 2.00.

Jim Pastorius was Brooklyn's leader in games won with sixteen. The left-hander, out of Pittsburgh, in only his second year in the Major Leagues, seemed destined for stardom, but with records of 4-20 and 1-9 in the next two years, his career came to an early end. Nap Rucker was the real ace of the staff. He won fifteen games and led the club in ERA, with a 2.06, and strikeouts, 131. It was a brilliant start for the rookie from Crabapple, Georgia, who remained with Brooklyn for his entire career (1907-1916).

The Dodgers closed out a mediocre season in appropriate fashion by being no-hit in September. Nick Maddoz of Pittsburgh was the hurler. He won twenty games the following year for the Pirates, but was back, in the minors by 1909.

Dodgers		**1907**	**Giants**	
Tim Jordan	.274	**BA**	Cy Seymour	.294
Harry Lumley	66	**RBI**	" "	75
" "	9	**HR**	George Browne	5
Jim Pastorius	16	**WINS**	Christy Mathewson	24*
Nap Rucker	2.06	**ERA**	" " "	2.00
" "	131	**SO**	" " "	178*

* led the National League

1908

Merkle's Infamous Mental Lapse

1908 was even worse for the Dodgers. They sank to seventh place, barely winning fifty-three games, while the Giants roared back to challenge the mighty Cubs. The regular season actually ended in a tie between the two teams, but the Cubs prevailed in the replay of a previously tied game. That game, and the events that required it, will live forever in baseball lore.

To achieve the final victory, the Cubs had to beat the Giants ace, Christy Mathewson, on the Giants home field – which they did by a score of 4-2. The scene for that playoff game on October 8th resembled a madhouse. Over 40,000 spectators may have seen some parts of the contest. "The New York Times" first ever coverage of a sporting event gushed, on page one: "Perhaps never in the history of a great city, since the days of Rome and its arena contests, has a people been pitched to such a key of excitement as was New York *fandom*." Cowbells, trumpets and fog horns resounded throughout the game. At one point, a mob of fans, who held tickets but could not be fit into old Manhattan Field, charged across the grounds and knocked down a portion of the back fence. One man actually died as a result of the hysteria. In order to get a look at the action, he had climbed a viaduct pillar, lost his grip and fallen to his death.

The tie game replay was necessitated by the most famous mental lapse in baseball history – Fred Merkle's failure to touch second base after an apparent game-winning hit. That win would have given the Giants the pennant. After the hit, as the crowd poured onto the field, Merkle, who had been on first, cut across the diamond toward the dugout instead of touching second base. (In his

31

defense, players often did this to avoid the unruly crowds at the end of an exciting game, but rarely was this breach of the rules acted upon.)

In this case, however, players on both teams began fighting with both spectators and each other for the ball, when it became apparent that the non-touching of second base was to become an issue. Finally, Johnny Evers, the Cubs second baseman, got the ball and stepped on second base for the force-out on Merkle. Since the rules clearly state that a run can not score if a force-out results in the third out, the game was still officially tied. Darkness descended and, inadvertently, as events played themselves out, Merkle's failure to touch second base cost the Giants a pennant.

As an additional sidelight to this exciting race, on October 8th, an amazing string of victories concluded when the Cubs Three-Finger Brown outdueled Christy Mathewson for the ninth consecutive time. Actually, in head-to-head competition, Brown beat Matty thirteen time in twenty-four tries. When we add the fact that the Cubs shortstop, Joe Tinker, had an uncanny knack for hitting Mathewson, we can begin to understand the difficulty facing McGraw in besting Frank Chance's boys.

The playoff game was a wild finish to a season that also saw Pittsburgh in contention until the very last day. They closed the season with the same 98-56 record as the Giants and finished in second place when the Giants lost the suspended game.

It was a year that also saw a three-team race in the American League. Detroit had to beat third-place Chicago on the last day of the season to win by a half-game over Cleveland. The two races exhausted players, fans and writers alike.

Through it all, Mathewson was magnificent. He posted thirty-seven wins in a losing cause to lead the league. He also was first in games started, appearances, complete games, innings pitched and strikeouts. Hooks Witse, out of Hamilton, N.Y., added twenty-three wins for New York.

Mike Donlin led the club with a .334 batting average. In an interesting sidelight, Donlin became probably the only player ever to be ejected from a game for protesting the granting of a base on balls. Apparently, he had urgent business elsewhere than the ballpark and preferred to be struck out. We can be sure that McGraw was pleased.

Meanwhile, the mediocre Brooklyn pitching staff led the league in issuing bases on ball with 444. (The Giants staff walked 288.) Brooklyn's Nap Walker managed to issue the most passes in the National League (125).

The Dodgers one bright note was Tim Jordan's topping of the league in home runs with twelve. It was a total that surpassed the year's production of eleven by the entire Philadelphia club!

The Brooklyn team of 1908 did set a record – one that all of their fans would like to forget. Their team batting average of .213 still stands as the worst in modern Major League history. Their best hitter, the same Tim Jordan, a New York City native, *led* the club with a .247 batting average! The Giants had almost 300 more hits than Brooklyn and a team batting average that was fifty-four points higher. Even for the dead ball era, Brooklyn's performance was dismal.

On a historical note, in 1908 the Dodgers acquired a journeyman right-handed pitcher named Kaiser Wilhelm (not a misprint). After being out of the Major Leagues for two years, he surprised everyone by posting a remarkable 1.87 ERA in forty-two appearances. He was thirty-four at the time. Wilhelm had gone 5-3 with Pittsburgh in 1903 and had also spent two years with the National League's Boston Beaneaters, where he recorded a 15-21 total in his first year, but slumped terribly in 1905 to 4-23. After two years in the ill-fated Federal League (1914-15), he dropped out of sight. This was probably fortunate, given his name and the anti-war hysteria that began to sweep the nation in 1917. The lad, actually from Wooster, Ohio, returned to manage the talentless Phillies in midseason of 1921. Kaiser lasted another full year and then he and his famous name vanished from baseball for good.

Dodgers		1908	Giants	
Tim Jordan	.247	**BA**	Mike Donlin	.334
" "	60	**RBI**	Mike Donlin	106
" "	12*	**HR**	" "	6
Nap Rucker	17	**WINS**	Christy Mathewson	37*
Kaiser Wilhelm	1.87	**ERA**	" " "	1.43*
Nap Rucker	199	**SO**	" " "	259*

* led the National League

1909

Zack Wheat Arrives in Brooklyn

In 1909, the Brooklyn club moved up a notch to sixth place. Meanwhile, the Giants dropped to third, twelve games behind the stunned Cubs – who, despite winning 104 games, still finished eight and a half games behind the Pirates! Those 104 wins set a record for a runner-up team that still stands.

This was the year that baseball had to endure the suicide of the National League president, Harry S. Pulliam, but it was also the year of Ty Cobb. Cobb won the American League's Triple Crown, leading in batting average, home runs and runs batted in. He also took honors in: slugging average, hits, total bases, runs scored and stolen bases. On the negative side, Cobb's combative nature also led to his indictment for assaulting a Cleveland night watchman. It was quite a year for the future hall-of-famer.

Another highlight of 1909 was the construction of the first all-concrete-and-steel stadiums to replace the typical wooden ballpark. The modern new parks were: Forbes Field in Pittsburgh and Shibe Park in Philadelphia.

Christy Mathewson had another banner year for the Giants. His 1.14 ERA led the league and he tied for best winning percentage with Pirate hurler Howie Camnitz by posting a 25-6 record.

Brooklyn's highlight for the year may have come on opening day against the Giants. The Dodgers were no-hit for nine innings by the Giants Red Ames, but managed to win the game in the thirteenth inning by scoring three runs for a 3-0 victory. It was mostly downhill after that. In a more appropriate vein for this lackluster club, their catcher, Bill Bergen, hit .139 in 112 games – the lowest batting average ever recorded for a regular player who was not a pitcher. (Apparently, at age thirty-six, Bill was such a savvy handler of pitchers, that the team could overlook his "hitting.")

Bergen was not the only weak spot in the Brooklyn lineup. Pryor (Humpy) McElveen appeared in eighty-five games, batted 258 times and hit a resounding .198. Joe Kustus, a "slugging" outfielder hit .145 in fifty-three games. Only an excellent pitching performance by the Dodgers four starters brought this club home in sixth-place.

Not one Brooklyn batter reached .300. John Hummel, nicknamed "Silent John," had one of the team's loudest bats. The Bloomsburg, Pennsylvania lad, who spent eleven years with Brooklyn, led the club with a .280 batting average; in runs batted in with fifty-two, and in home runs with four. All of this while alternating at four positions. The following year, he became the regular second baseman.

His counterpart on the Giants, Larry Doyle, led his team with a .302 batting average, while Red Murray drove in ninety-one runs and hit a league-leading seven homers.

As one might surmise from their third place finish, the Giants outpitched their cross-town rivals. Their pitchers led both leagues with 695 strikeouts. Their staff ERA was 2.27, compared to Brooklyn's 3.10. At the plate, while the Giants hit only ten more home runs than did the Dodgers, they knocked in 140 more runs.

The Brooklyn staff's ERA's are somewhat misleading. Actually, Bell, Rucker, Scanlan and Hunter all had ERA's under 3.00. It was the rest of the staff that ballooned the team ERA to over 3.00. Rucker almost led the National League in strikeouts, with 201. He fell only four short of the Cub's unusually named hurler, Orvie Overall. They were close, however, only in the strikeout statistic. Orvie won twenty games for the Cubs, while Rucker lost nineteen for Brooklyn.

There was a ray of hope for Brooklyn, though. A twenty-two-year-old, left-handed batting outfielder named Zack Wheat, out of Hamilton, Missouri, was brought up late in the year to bolster the feeble attack. He played in twenty-six games and hit .304. Zack would star for Brooklyn until 1927, when the club outraged its fans by selling him to the Philadelphia club of the American League. In his final year as an active player, at age forty-one, Zack showed that he could still hit by batting .324 in eighty-eight games.

Dodgers		1909	Giants	
John Hummel	.280	**BA**	Larry Doyle	.302
" "	52	**RBI**	Red Murray	91
" "	4	**HR**	" "	7*
George Bell	16	**WINS**	Christy Mathewson	25
Nap Rucker	2.24	**ERA**	" " "	1.14*
" "	201	**SO**	" " "	149

* led the National League

1910

The Cubs Outlast the Giants

1910 was almost an exact replica of the previous year for Brooklyn. They were sixth again, with the same batting average that they recorded in 1909 – another mediocre .229. They were fortunate that St. Louis and Boston were even more inept, especially in the area of pitching, which once again saved Brooklyn from sinking even further in the standings. The Dodgers won nine more games than in 1909 (64 as compared to 55).

There was hope for the future though – and perhaps the birth of their famous slogan – "Wait 'till next year!" The livelier, cork-centered ball was invented in 1910. It would put an end to the dead ball era and the dominance of pitchers. Playing in a small park, as they did, a livelier ball might help them more in the future than a continuing reliance upon great pitching. (This proved to be especially true for Brooklyn in the 1950's.)

The cork-centered ball was invented by Ben Shibe, (not the same Shibe that the Phillies park was named for) and experimented with in the 1910 World Series. The powerful Philadelphia Athletics proceeded to crush the Chicago Cubs in five games, while averaging seven runs per outing. The owners were convinced and the ball was adopted for use by both leagues in the following year. 1910 was also the first year that a U.S. President (Taft) would throw out the first ball to open the season. Baseball had truly arrived as the national pastime.

Chicago won the pennant, and the Giants clawed their way up to second-place, past a tough Pittsburgh team. Brooklyn batters held the dubious distinction of striking out a league-leading number of times, but the Giants bats were smoking. They scored an incredible 218 more runs than their cross-town rivals (715 to 497) and had a team batting average almost fifty points higher (.275 to .229). Their slugging average was also more than sixty points better!

The Giants dominated the pitching statistics, led by Christie Mathewson's National League best of 27 wins. He also had a lower ERA and more strikeouts than anyone on the Brooklyn staff. The Giants staff struck out a league-leading 717, as compared to 555 for Brooklyn.

Nap Rucker did his part for Brooklyn. The Crabapple, Georgia native led the staff with seventeen victories and, as the staff workhorse, led the league in games started (39), complete games (27) and innings pitched (320). Unfortunately, he also led the league in hits given up – 293, which averaged out to almost one an inning.

Mathewson, by comparison, pitched two innings less than Rucker and gave up only one less hit. It may be fair to claim that had the two pitchers changed teams at the beginning of the season, their won-lost records might have been reversed.

The Dodgers were obviously much slower afoot than the Giants. The Giants stole 282 bases to their 151. Also, they did not have a single .300 hitter, again, while the Giants boasted two. Fred Snodgrass hit .321 and a rookie outfielder, Josh Devore, batted .304.

A telling statistic reveals that, out of a Brooklyn pitching staff of eleven arms, only Rucker and George Bell managed to strike out more batters than they walked. In no sense were the Brooklyn batters capable of overcoming such a disadvantage.

It was clearly a difficult year for the Brooklyn club's new manager, Bill Dahlen. He had just turned forty. The previous year, at the ripe old age of thirty-nine for a player, he had played 39 games as a utility infielder for Boston. His slugging average of .305 was better than that of half of the regulars on his new team. Dahlen could hit. In 1908, he also had had a respectable (for the dead ball era) slugging average of .307. Perhaps Brooklyn should have made him a playing manager!

The first decade of the twentieth century had ended. It had started brilliantly for Brooklyn with a pennant and two first-division finishes, while the Giants had been last twice and with a seventh-place finish in the first three years. The rest of the decade saw a complete reversal, as Brooklyn finished in the second division every year from 1904 to 1910, while the Giants either won the pennant or finished in the first division. The next decade would find the competition between the two clubs a bit more even.

Dodgers		1910	Giants	
Zack Wheat	.284	**BA**	Fred Snodgrass	.321
John Hummel	74	**RBI**	Red Murray	87
Jake Daubert	8	**HR**	Larry Doyle	8
Nap Rucker	17	**WINS**	Christy Mathewson	27*
" "	2.59	**ERA**	" " "	1.90
" "	147	**SO**	" " "	184

* led the National League

1911

The Giants Win the Pennant

In 1911, the Giants and the Phillies became the first major League teams to wear white "home" and dark "visitors" uniforms. The idea soon became popular and eventually mandatory in both leagues.

1911 also saw Brooklyn spend its ninth consecutive year in the second division. In fact, they slumped to seventh place, despite winning the same sixty-four games that they had won in the previous year. A rejuvenated St. Louis team won twelve more games than they did in 1910 and "leaped" from seventh to fifth place in the standings. Fortunately, for the Dodgers, Boston remained inept – winning only forty-four games to finish twenty and a half games behind Brooklyn. Boston managed to set a record for the worst performance in home games that still stands! They won only nineteen of seventy-three games in their own park.

Jake Daubert, the pride of Shamokin, Pennsylvania, and the durable first baseman for Brooklyn, became their first .300 hitter since Harry Lumley and Jack McCarthy turned the trick in 1906. Unfortunately, his teammates managed to lead the league in striking out, once again, with a total of 683 whiffs. One Brooklyn outfielder, Bob Coulson, tied for the league lead in strikeouts with seventy-eight in 521 at bats. Since he also hit .234 with no home runs, it was no surprise that he did not return in 1912.

On the mound, Nap Rucker once again starred for the Dodgers. He led the club with twenty-two wins, an ERA of 2.72 and 190 strikeouts. No other starter had a winning record.

Meanwhile, in stark contrast to the dismal goings-on at Brooklyn's home games, the Polo Grounds rocked as John McGraw led his Giants past the Cubs and Pirates to capture the National League flag by seven and a half games. Despite losing to Connie Mack's Athletics in the World Series, the Giants had had a great year. They led the league in batting average, slugging average, runs batted in and stolen bases. Their 373 stolen bases is still a team record.

Their pitching staff posted league-leading ERA's, led in strikeouts, complete games and, as might be expected of a pennant winner, winning percentage. One standout was Rube Marquard, from Cleveland, Ohio. He was purchased for $11,000 from the Indianapolis club (the largest sum to that date ever paid for a player), but had been a bust in his first two years as a Giant. In fact, after going 9-17 during that period, he began being referred to by the sportswriters as "the $11,000 lemon." All of that changed when, on a May day in 1911, with Mathewson on the mound to start the game against the Cardinals, the Giants shocked them, and probably themselves, by scoring thirteen runs in the first inning. McGraw decided that, with such a lead, he might as well give his ace a rest and give Marquard some work. "Maybe, Rube can get someone out," he was recalled to say. Rube did. He struck out fourteen Cardinals in eight innings, regained his confidence, and went on to post a 24-7 won-lost record while leading the league in strikeouts with 237. Thus are managerial and pitching legends sometimes born in baseball.

The Giants pitching staff's fine record is especially notable when one realizes that this was the first full year for the lively, cork-centered (rabbit) ball. Over in the American League, for example, Ty Cobb hit an amazing .420 to set a Major League record that still stands. The Giants also enjoyed pounding the new ball: their second baseman, Larry Doyle, cracked twenty-five triples – still a record for second basemen. He also scored 102 runs to lead the club.

His colleague on the right side of the infield, first baseman, Fred Merkle, also took advantage of the lively ball. In the first inning of a game on May 13th, he drove in six runs to set a record that stood until 1970, when another Giant, this time in a San Francisco uniform, Jim Hart, matched the feat.

Unfortunately, in a six game World Series, watched by a record breaking 180,000, the Giants bats fell silent against the talented pitching staff of the Philadelphia Athletics. They hit only .175. Still, they had made it to the World Series for the first time since 1905. Fate decreed, however, that this would be the last hurrah for the old Polo Grounds. It burned down after the season and had to be completely rebuilt.

Students of baseball lore will recall that it was in this World Series that, much to the chagrin of manager John McGraw, both Marquard and Mathewson, despite direct instructions to the contrary, each threw a high fast ball to the Athletics Frank Baker in two consecutive games. Baker belted both pitches over the right field fence to forever earn the nickname: "Home Run" Baker. In reality, he had hit only eleven homers in 1911 and hit only two in 1910. While Baker did lead the American League with ten in 1912 and twelve in 1913, he hit only nine in 1914 and retired to work his farm at the end of the season.

Baker reappeared with the New York Yankees seven years later and clouted a total of sixteen homes for them in the 1921 and 1922 campaigns before retiring for good. He had a career total of ninety-six four-baggers. However, before we sniff disdainfully at that total, let us not lose sight of the fact that Baker achieved his fame in an era, not only of dead balls, but with pitchers throwing shiners, spitballs, nicked and discolored balls and with full authority to do almost anything with the baseball to keep a batter from hitting it. In retrospect, the nickname was well deserved.

The great Cy Young was traded to the Braves by Cleveland in mid-season. He won the last four of his amazing 511 victories for

43

that last place club and retired at age forty-four. Twenty-four years later, Babe Ruth would conclude his fabulous career with those same Braves. They finished in last place too.

Dodgers		1911	Giants	
Jake Daubert	.307	**BA**	Chief Meyers	.332
Zack Wheat	76	**RBI**	Fred Merkle	84
Tex Erwin	7	**HR**	Larry Doyle	13
Nap Rucker	22	**WINS**	Christy Mathewson	26
" "	2.72	**ERA**	" " "	1.99*
" "	190	**SO**	Rube Marquard	237*

* led the National League

1912

Another Winner for McGraw

1912 brought no relief for Brooklyn. They finished seventh again and missed being a cellar club only by the good graces of Boston, which managed to lose at least 100 games for the fourth consecutive year. The Dodgers, by comparison, lost "only" ninety-five. Jake Daubert and Zack Wheat made contact with the lively ball often enough to bat over .300, but the team still finished a woeful 46 games behind the pennant-winning Giants. A brash youngster named Casey Stengel appeared in seventeen games, hit .316 and thus became a regular the following year. Nap Rucker won eighteen games for the Dodgers, while losing twenty-one. No other hurler won more than seven! Ruckers' ERA of 2.21 was the only ERA under 3.36 on the squad.

At the Polo Grounds, John McGraw's awesome club led the league in batting average, runs-batted-in, home runs (47), runs scored and stolen bases. Larry Doyle had an even better year than in 1911. He hit .330 with 90 RBI's and was voted the coveted Chalmers award as the league's best player. The award included a beautiful, new Chalmers automobile.

As if their powerful lineup was not enough, the Giants pitchers had the league's lowest ERA and the highest winning percentage. It is no wonder that they finished ten games ahead of Honus Wagner's Pirates. They scored 172 more runs than Brooklyn did and had a team batting average that was eighteen points higher. Their pitchers walked 172 less batters and struck out 99 more than did the Brooklyn staff.

45

As usual, Christy Mathewson starred for the Giants. He had a 23-12 record. A 23-year-old youngster with a wicked spitter, Jeff Tesreau, had an ERA below 2.00 to lead the National League and threw a no-hitter against the Phillies. But it was once again Rube Marquard who startled the baseball world by winning 19 consecutive games from April 11th to July 3rd. He ended with a league-leading 26 wins. His streak tied the record of another Giant, Tim Keefe, who had won 19 straight back in 1888. Actually, if modern scoring rules had been in effect, Marquard would have won 20 consecutive games. He relieved Tesreau on July 4th after defeating Brooklyn 2-1 for his nineteenth straight victory on July 3rd. He had entered the game with the Giants trailing, but, although they went on to win, the rules at the time gave the victory to Tesreau as the starting pitcher. Perhaps, like Roger Maris, Marquard should get an asterisk next to his name in the record book.

Chief Meyers out of Riverside, California, was the Giants leading hitter, with a .358 BA and Red Murray led the club with 92 RBI's. In addition to his league-leading 26 wins, Marquard led the club with 175 strikeouts. Nap Rucker was once again the leader for Brooklyn in wins, ERA and strikeouts. Unfortunately, he lacked support and ended up with a mediocre 18-21 won-lost record. It was the second consecutive year that Brooklyn's Daubert and New York's Meyers led their clubs in hitting, and the first time in six years that Mathewson did not lead the Giants pitchers in either wins, ERA or strikeouts. He would be back on top in 1913.

The Giants met the Red Sox in a wild World Series that featured eight thrilling games (One game was a tie called by darkness) and included a bare-handed catch of what should have been a Giants home run by Red Sox outfielder Harry Hooper. The Giants lost the series four games to three, but it will always be remembered for Giants outfielder Fred Snodgrass' unfortunate drop of a fly ball in the tenth inning of the final game. It became known as the "$30,000 muff," reflecting the winner's share that it cost the Giants. That "muff" overshadowed the amazing performance of New York's Buck Herzog, who set a World Series record by getting twelve hits! Christy Mathewson allowed only four earned runs in 28.2 innings, but ended up 0-2 as everything seemed to go the Red Sox' way. Mathewson was 0-2 with a 1.26 ERA, while the Red Sox star, Smokey Joe Wood, won three games with an ERA of 3.68! As any Red Sox fan will attest, however, their teams' luck has evened up over the years.

McGraw's rage at losing the World Series overflowed against Coach Wilbert Robinson. They quarreled and, despite five years of loyal service, McGraw gave him the ax. Robinson would gain some measure of revenge by managing Brooklyn over the Giants in 1915, 1916 and 1920. They finally reconciled many years later.

That winter, John McGraw went on tour. He actually became the highest paid performer in all of vaudeville when his baseball talks earned him the stupendous sum, for its time, of $3,000 a week for fifteen weeks! Even Al Jolson was not earning that kind of money.

Dodgers	1912		Giants	
Jake Daubert	.308	**BA**	Chief Meyers	.358
" "	66	**RBI**	Red Murray	92
Zack Wheat	8	**HR**	Fred Merkle	11
Nap Rucker	18	**WINS**	Rube Marquard	26*
" "	2.21	**ERA**	Jeff Tesreau	1.96*
" "	151	**SO**	Rube Marquard	175

* led the National League

The official flag raising for the first game at a brand new Ebbets
Field on a chilly April 9, 1913.

1913

Ebbets Field Opens

1913 saw Brooklyn inch their way back up to sixth-place. An amazing resurgence by Boston had them leaping from their customary last-place finish to fifth, while Cincinnati, under its new manager – player-manager Joe Tinker, of Tinker to Evers to Chance fame – fell from fourth the previous year to seventh. St. Louis, with a dreadful 51 and 99 mark finished dead last.

St. Louis featured second baseman Miller Huggins as player-manager. (He had hit .304 in 1912 at age thirty-three.) He would end his career with the Cardinals four years later, just as a young shortstop named Rogers Hornsby was beginning his. In 1918, Huggins became the manager of the New York Yankees and would remain in that position until his death in September of 1929 at age sixty. Miller would take the Cardinals to third place in 1914, be back in the cellar by 1916, and then drive them back to third in 1917 before beginning his storied career with the pinstripers – highlighted by his ongoing problems with the incorrigible Babe Ruth.

The big news in Brooklyn was the opening of Ebbets Field and Jake Daubert's league-leading .350 batting average. Ebbets Field was officially opened on April 9th. Built on 4½ acres of filled in swampland, on the lowest slope of Crown Heights that was affectionately called "pigtown," the park was supposed to hold a capacity of 32,000. Technically, the fire department prohibited more than 33,000 spectators. It should be noted that on August 30, 1947, 37,512 fans "unofficially" were in Ebbets Field to watch the Dodgers go against the Giants.

49

Zack Wheat hit .301 and third baseman, Red Smith (no relation to the famed sportswriter), led the league with forty doubles. The Dodgers offense was decent, but their pitching staff failed them once again. Pat Ragan's fifteen wins led the club, but he lost eighteen. Rucker also lost more games than he won. Other than these two, no Brooklyn hurler won more than eight games.

Despite all of the excitement in Brooklyn, it was once again, a Giants year. They won the pennant by 12½ games over a surprising Phillies team. The Giants had fewer home runs than the five teams directly below them in the standings (Even the Dodgers, with 39, topped the Giants 31), but they could play the game. They led the league in batting average with a .273 mark and stolen bases with 296.

On the mound, Mathewson, Marquard and Tesreau all won more than 20 games, and started 106 games between the three of them. The staff's ERA was the league's best at 2.43 (compared to Brooklyn's 3.13 and the second-place Phillie's 3.16). Mathewson led all National League pitchers with a nifty 2.06 ERA. At one point, he went a startling, and record setting, 68 innings without giving up a walk! This feat was not duplicated for sixty-three years, until Randy Jones of the San Diego padres did it in 1976. Mathewson finished with an incredible 0.62 walks-per-game average for the year.

The Giants scored 121 more runs than did Brooklyn, but, surprisingly, their team batting average was only three points higher. Their slugging average, however, topped Brooklyn's by over 100 points.

Once again, McGraw and his Giants were to be disappointed in the Fall Classic. They fell to the powerful Philadelphia Athletics, four games to one. Injuries played a part and their depleted lineup managed only a puny .201 batting average in the series.

Dodgers		1913	Giants	
Jake Daubert	.350*	**BA**	Chief Meyers	.312
George Cutshaw	80	**RBI**	Larry Doyle	73
" " " " Casey Stengel Zack Wheat	7	**HR**	" " " " Tillie Shafer	5
Pat Ragan	15	**WINS**	Christy Mathewson	25
Ed Reulbach	2.05	**ERA**	" " "	2.06*
Nap Rucker	111	**SO**	Jeff Tesreau	167

* led the National League

1914

Uncle "Robby" Arrives

The Dodgers climbed to fifth place in 1914, with their new manager, Wilbert Robinson, later to be known as "Uncle Robbie." Out of Bolton, Massachusetts, he had played in the old American Association. He moved to the Cardinals in 1900 and began his managerial career with Baltimore as the replacement for John McGraw in 1902 when McGraw grew weary of American League President Ban Johnson's harassment. As previously mentioned, Robinson was on the bench as a coach for the Giants when they blew the 1912 World Series to the Red Sox. "Uncle Robbie" would manage the Dodgers until 1931. He was reputed to have been a reliable catcher defensively, who had a way with pitchers. He was also a respectable hitter, compiling a lifetime batting average of .277 in over a thousand games and more than five thousand at-bats.

He also became known later as "Rotund Willie," among other things. It was said that he could not be bothered with details, and would leave a player's name off the lineup card if he had trouble spelling it. There were also complaints that he left players sitting on the bench for months, because he forgot that they were on the team! Still, from 1914 to 1931, under his leadership, the Dodgers won two pennants and finished in the first division seven times.

World War I had broken out in Europe and baseball had a war of its own on its hands when the Federal League set up shop as the third major league. (Brooklyn also had a team in that league and, coincidentally, it also came in fifth.)

John McGraw's Giants were once again the major story in New York. After three consecutive pennants, the Giants appeared poised to coast to a fourth, but it was not to be. Although Rube Marquard was losing more than he was winning, Mathewson and Tesreau were doing well and, by June, the Giants, as expected, were well ahead of the pack.

In last place as late as July 18th, the Boston Braves, a team of castoffs and "never-were's," suddenly started winning. By July 21st, they had moved up to fourth place. Inexplicably, they kept winning and, by August 12th, they were in second! With only one .300 hitter, and only three pitchers that manager George Stallings could count on, the Braves seemed to be more of an oddity than a threat to the Giants, at first. But miracles do happen, and, just as inexplicably, the Giants started losing. On September 2nd, the Braves actually moved into first place! By September 8th, they were in first place to stay. They had won 34 of 44 games during that stretch and they kept winning. To everyone's amazement, including, possibly, their own, the Braves finished 10 ½ games in front of the stunned Giants.

It was the greatest comeback in baseball history, and they capped their improbable year by crushing the heavily favored Philadelphia Athletics in the World Series in four straight games. (They played their home games in the Red Sox Park, Fenway Park, because it held more seats; but nothing mattered to this club, which was forever to be known as the "Miracle Braves.") The miracle did not last for long. By 1917, the Braves were back in the second division and finishing 25 ½ games behind the same Giants that they had ambushed in 1914.

Statistically, the Giants had a great year. They led the league in runs scored and stolen bases, and their pitching staff led in shutouts with twenty. One could point at Rube Marquard as part of the reason for the Giants late-season fade. He slumped to a record of only 12 wins as against 22 losses. This, from a pitcher who had sparkled the year before with a record of 23-10. Tesreau was 26-10 and Mathewson was productive at 24-13, but the rest of the staff was mediocre. Tesreau led the league with eight shutouts and forty starts. George Burns (.303) was the only Giants regular to hit over .300. He had led the league in striking out (74) the previous year. Fred Merkle took the "honors" in 1914 whiffing eighty times.

The Dodgers captured fifth-place by a single game over Philadelphia. Surprisingly, they led the league in team batting with a .269 average, and their pitching staff had a lower ERA than did the second-place Giants – 2.82 to 2.94. However, only hurler Jeff Pfeffer won 20 games (he was 23-12). Raleigh Atchison was next best with a mere 12 wins. A highlight for Brooklyn was the performance of a 23-year-old outfielder named Casey Stengel. He hit .316 and led the league in on-base percentage with a .404.

With four .300 hitters in the lineup, one of them the league's leading hitter, Jake Daubert (.329,) Brooklyn was beginning to show some life. Unfortunately, one of their .300 hitters, Jack Dalton, jumped to the new Federal League's Buffalo franchise at season's end and never returned. (He played eight games for Detroit in the American League in 1916 and was finished as an active major leaguer.)

1914 was also notable for two other events. The New York team in the American League began being called the Yankees, and a 19-year-old kid named Babe Ruth made his major league debut for the Red Sox by pitching seven innings to beat Cleveland on July 1st. He pitched very little that year – only 23 innings – and finished with a 2-1 record. In 1915, at the tender age of twenty, he would win 18 games for the Sox.

Dodgers		1914	Giants	
Jake Daubert	.329*	**BA**	George Burns	.303
Zack Wheat	89	**RBI**	Art Fletcher	79
" "	9	**HR**	Fred Merkle	7
Jeff Pfeffer	23	**WINS**	Jeff Tesreau	26
" "	1.97	**ERA**	" "	2.38
" "	135	**SO**	" "	189

* led the National League

1915

Robby's Boys Gain 1st Division

Wilbert Robinson, much to everyone's surprise, led a "starless" Brooklyn team to a third-place finish, ending a string of twelve consecutive years in the second-division. It also marked the first time that the Dodgers had ended up higher in the standings than the Giants since 1902! Coincidentally, the Giants finished last in that year, just as they did in 1915.

Nothing went right for the Giants. Mathewson seemed a lot older than his chronological age of 34; his tired right arm produced only 8 wins against 14 losses, and his ERA leaped .58 from 3.00 in 1914. The low point of a cheerless season probably came on August 31st, when Jimmy Lavender of the Cubs no-hit them. It was definitely the highlight of Jimmy's six-year career in the big leagues. He won 63 and lost 76 for the Cubs and Phillies before retiring.

Jeff Tesreau, from Silver Mine, Missouri, was once again the ace of the Giants staff in 1915. He posted a 19-16 record and an ERA of only 2.29. This was in contrast to the fact that the Giants pitching staff gave up more hits than any other team in the league – 1,350.

Their production at the plate was also down dramatically. On the one hand, they led the league with 501 RBI's; on the other hand, they had driven in 65 more runs the year before. They also scored 90 less runs than they did in the previous year and once more could boast only one .300 hitter. Larry Doyle not only led the club, but he led the league with a .320 mark. He also led the league in hits (189) and doubles with 40.

Clearly, the Giants were a team of contrasts. Tesreau and Doyle had excellent years, the team led in RBI's and, even by finishing last, the Giants set a record. They finished only 21 games behind the first-place Phillies. No last-place team would ever be closer to the pennant winner in modern baseball history until the expansion of both leagues into divisions.

To fully appreciate Wilbert Robinson's accomplishment in leading Brooklyn to a first-division finish, it should be noted that they scored 86 less runs than in the previous year; their team batting average slipped from .269 in 1914 to .248; their slugging average went from .355 to .317 and they hit only 14 home runs as compared to 31 in 1914. (They were last in the NL in this category.) Jake Daubert was the their only .300 hitter and no hurler won twenty games. Indeed, if the Phillies had not vaulted from sixth-place in 1914 to the pennant in 1915, Robinson could well have been manager-of-the-year. To make things even more difficult for him, he got little help from Casey Stengel who slipped from .316 in 1914 to .237 in 1915.

This was the last year for the Federal League. Its collapse enabled the two major leagues to look forward to a year of player stability in 1916.

Dodgers		1915	Giants	
Jake Daubert	.301	**BA**	Larry Doyle	.320*
Zack Wheat	66	**RBI**	Art Fletcher	74
" "	5	**HR**	Larry Doyle Fred Merkle	4
Jeff Pfeffer	19	**WINS**	Jeff Tesreau	19
" "	2.10	**ERA**	" "	2.29
Wheezer Dell	94	**SO**	" "	176

* led the National League

Chief Meyers, Wilbert Robinson and Rube Marquard at Spring
Training on April 5, 1916. The Dodgers were to take the pennant in
Uncle "Robby's" third year at the helm.

1916

Brooklyn Wins the Pennant

1916 was a truly miraculous year for the Dodgers. Having made their initial appearance in the first division since 1902 the previous year, no one expected, after all of those dismal seasons that the Brooklyn club, now commonly referred to as the "Robins" after their popular manager would actually capture the National League flag in 1916. Somehow they did, but it wasn't easy.

As late as the last week of the season, the Phillies and Boston were still in contention; however, the schedule favored Brooklyn. Philadelphia and Boston were forced to play a pair of doubleheaders against each other and succeeded in knocking themselves out of the race. The Phillies featured Grover Cleveland Alexander, who won thirty-three games, threw sixteen shutouts and had an ERA of 1.55! Even so, the Beantowners probably would have won it all, if injuries had not plagued their top players.

Zack Wheat led Brooklyn with nine home runs and a .312 batting average. He also excited fans with a twenty-nine game hitting streak. Old reliable Jake Daubert, now thirty-two years old, hit .316; but it was Brooklyn's pitching staff that was truly outstanding. They topped the league with an ERA of 2.12. Pfeffer won twenty-five games and the staff combined for twenty-two shutouts. They also led the league in hits with 1,366, thirty more than runner-up Cincinnati, but, more importantly, over one hundred more than either Philadelphia or Boston.

In just three short years at the helm, Wilbert Robinson (Uncle Robbie) had taken over a team mired in the second division for more than a decade, and brought them a pennant. Whatever might be said about him in the future, and there was much criticism, he had delivered.

The Giants had a sort of miracle year of their own, despite a fourth-place finish in the league standings. They lost eight straight games at home at the start, then went on the road and won seventeen consecutive contests. When they slumped again, manager John McGraw decided not to wait until the end of the season and began to rebuild the club in midsummer.

Former ace, Christy Mathewson was released so that he could become manager of the woeful Cincinnati club. McGraw then traded Bill McKechnie (later to manage that same Cincinnati club, but with more success than Mathewson), Larry Doyle and Fred Merkle. The fans howled, but the new blood, that included infielder Heinie Zimmerman from the Cubs, inspired the club. They made a sensational rush to the finish line in September – at one point, winning twenty-six consecutive home games – but it wasn't enough. When they lost to Boston on September 30th, it left them with a fourth place finish, only seven games behind pennant-winning Brooklyn.

Pol Perritt, out of Arcadia, Louisiana, led the Giants staff with an 18-11 mark. Rube Benton was 16-8 and Jeff Tesreau was 14-14. All three had ERA's below 3.00, but no one else on the staff won as many as ten games. At bat, Dave Robertson led the league in home runs with twelve. The revamped Giants led the league in runs batted in, runs scored and stolen bases. A twenty-game winner on the pitching staff could have made the difference for this team. As it was, Brooklyn got their long awaited pennant.

Unfortunately, although the National League had a different entry in this year's World Series, the American League sent back the Boston Red Sox and the result was the same. The National League club fell in five games. The Red Sox' great pitching stifled the Brooklyn bats – they hit only .200 over the five game series. In Game Two, a beefy left-hander for the Red Sox, named Babe Ruth, pitched all fourteen innings for a 2-1 victory. Ruth also happened to be the American League's ERA leader with a 1.75. He won twenty-three games and set a record for southpaws by hurling nine shutouts. Oh yes, he could hit a little too, although he went 0-5 in the Series. (Sherry Smith, out of Monticello, Georgia, who had won fourteen games for Brooklyn during the regular season, was the hard luck loser to Ruth in that second game of the Series.)

Dodgers		**1916**	**Giants**	
Jake Daubert	.316	**BA**	Dave Robertson	.307
Zack Wheat	73	**RBI**	Bennie Kauff	74
" "	9	**HR**	Dave Robertson	12*
Jeff Pfeffer	25	**WINS**	Pol Perritt	18
Rube Marquard	1.58	**ERA**	" "	2.62
Larry Cheney	166	**SO**	Pol Perritt	115
			Rube Benton	

* led the National League

The slick infield that helped bring Brooklyn the pennant in 1916 *(left to right):* Jake Daubert, George Cutshaw, Ivy Olson and Harry Mowrey.

1917

McGraw Creates Another Winner

The remaking of the Giants that John McGraw had accomplished in midseason of 1916 paid off handsomely in 1917 as the Giants coasted to the National League pennant. They had a new look at the plate with Heinie Zimmerman, who led the league in RBI's with 102, George Burns, the leader in runs scored with 103, and Dave Robertson tying with Garvy Cravath of the Phillies for the league lead in home runs with twelve.

The Giants also led the league as a team in runs scored (635), but, just as importantly, their pitching staff allowed the fewest runs (457). Four Giants starters won at least fifteen games and three of them (Schupp, Perritt and Anderson) were in the top five of the National League's ERA leaders. Anderson led the club with a 1.44 ERA. Ferdie Schupp "slumped" to a 1.95 – he had posted a remarkable ERA of 0.90 in 1916 in eleven starts.

Their brilliant season was somewhat dimmed by shoddy play in the World Series. Dropped fly balls, careless run-downs that allowed Chicago White Sox runners to escape being picked off and other mental errors, so untypical of a McGraw managed team, wasted a dramatic comeback on their part. Down two games to none, the Giants got consecutive shutouts from Benton and Schupp to tie the Series; but the White Sox won the next two games to take the championship. It was McGraw's fourth consecutive World Series loss after winning in his first try in 1906.

Meanwhile, after being the Cinderella team of 1916, the Brooklyn club slumped to seventh place. Wilbert Robinson's early, magic touch could not compensate for a team that was starting to badly show its age. Four of the eight starting pitchers were in their thirties and the team was beginning to show an alarming propensity for losing close games in the late innings.

Rube Marquard was the only hurler for Brooklyn to finish above .500. He went 19-12. The staff's ERA ballooned from 2.12 the previous year to 2.78 in 1917.

Their hitters were aging too. Jake Daubert, now thirty-three, dropped from .316 the year before, to .261. Zack Wheat, at thirty-one, who had slugged fifty-six extra-base hits the previous year, had only twenty-seven this year. Still he led the club in batting with a .312 average. Wheat had not led the club in hitting since 1910, and it broke Jake Daubert's streak of being the team's batting leader for six consecutive years. Stengel and Hickman tied for the club's lead in home runs with six apiece.

1917 featured what many baseball purists call the greatest pitching performance in Major League history. On May 2, 1917, Hippo Vaughn of the Cubs and Fred Toney of Cincinnati both threw nine inning no-hitters at each other. It has never happened since. Actually, the game ended in the tenth inning, when a hit and a misjudged fly ball got the Reds shortstop, Larry Kopf, to third base. The "World's fastest human," as Jim Thorpe was billed, became the next batter. The Olympic hero, turned Major League ballplayer, lived up to his billing by beating out a dribbler to win the game for Cincinnati.

Speaking of Thorpe, he batted .247 in sixty-nine games for the Reds before being traded to the Giants. Clearly, he was signed as a crowd attraction, but McGraw was too much of a perfectionist to allow Thorpe's weak bat in the lineup very often. He let Thorpe pinch-run occasionally, but generally kept him out of the action. (Thorpe appeared in just twenty-six games for the Giants and batted a sickly .193.) In addition, despite his great speed and the accumulation of eleven hits, Thorpe stole only one base. As Michael Jordan would discover many decades later, having the physical skills to excel in one sport does not always guarantee success in another.

It should be noted that 1917 was the final year of Honus Wagner's legendary career. Unfortunately, for the "Flying Dutchman," it was the first time in the twentieth century that Pittsburgh finished in last place. Ironically, they would not finish in the cellar again for thirty years.

Dodgers	1917		Giants	
Zack Wheat	.312	**BA**	Benny Kauff	.308
Casey Stengel	73	**RBI**	Heinie Zimmerman	102*
Jim Hickman Casey Stengel	6	**HR**	Dave Robertson	12*
Rube Marquard	19	**WINS**	Ferdie Schupp	21
Jeff Pfeffer	2.23	**ERA**	Fred Anderson	1.44
Rube Marquard	117	**SO**	Ferdie Schupp	147

* led the National League

1918

World War I Takes its Toll

Hank Gowdy of the Braves had been the first Major Leaguer to enlist in "the war to end all wars," in June 1917. One year later, the "Work or fight" edict by Provost Marshall, General Crowder, boomed forth from our nation's capitol and forced draft-age men into either the military or designated essential industries. Many players were either drafted, enlisted or gained deferment through working in defense jobs. This put a large dent in the rosters of many a Major League club.

In addition, baseball had been ruled to be a nonessential industry and a shortened season ended on Labor Day, September 2nd. It actually took a "period of grace" from Secretary of War Baker to gain even this much of a concession. War fever had clearly taken over the country, but baseball was not completely forgotten.

Babe Ruth was the big story of 1918. He led the Red Sox to the pennant by, not only hitting .300 as a part-time player, or by belting eleven home runs to tie for the league lead, or even by adding an equal number of triples – the Babe could run – but by finding the time to start nineteen games and win thirteen of them. His ERA was a very respectable 2.22.

However, the Babe, being the Babe, was at his best when the spotlight was upon him and the World Series was the perfect vehicle. He pitched a shutout in Game One and extended his personal record of scoreless innings pitched in a World Series to twenty-nine and two/thirds. The Cubs finally scored a run off of him in the Fourth game, but the Red Sox were once again champions. In this pitchers series, a grand total of only nineteen runs were scored in the six games. Not a single home run was hit by either team! Even the Babe could not connect for one!

Meanwhile, as Ruth's star rose, baseball's other great performer, Ty Cobb, was not yet ready to sink into oblivion. At age thirty-one, Cobb won his eleventh batting title with a .382 average. He was also still spry enough, or dangerous enough with his flying spikes, to steal thirty-four bases. (Cobb would win his last batting crown the following year.)

Back in the National League, the Giants were left in the dust by 10 ½ games, but, in all fairness, they were badly hurt by loss of personnel due to the war. Their most productive hitter, Ross Youngs, batted .302. He also managed to lead the league by striking out forty-nine times. (That was considered a lot in the years before Ruth glamorized the home run and made striking out a hundred times a year acceptable.) With only two pitchers, Perritt and Causey (a rookie), able to win more than eight games, the Giants did well to finish second to the Cubs.

As the Giants were struggling on the baseball field, their ex-ace, Christy Mathewson, a captain in the army, was being overcome by poison gas at the front in France. Matty was thirty-eight years old – he would survive for only seven more years.

Their star pitcher for many years, Jeff Tesreau, was one of those who never returned to baseball after the war. He posted a 4-4 record in 1918 before gaining a deferment for entering an essential industry. Given the salaries and uncertainty of life in the Major Leagues, Tesreau opted to end his career at the age of twenty-nine.

For Brooklyn, it was an up and down season. One "highlight" occurred when Casey Stengel entered baseball folklore on his return to Ebbets Field after being traded to Pittsburgh in the off-season. In response to the welcoming cheers of the crowd, Casey doffed his cap and a sparrow flew out. The team moved up to fifth place, despite setting a National League record by losing nine games to start the season. Of some solace was the fact that they ended the streak by beating the Giants, 5-3, in the opening game of a doubleheader. A youthful Burleigh Grimes, out of Clear Lake, Wisconsin, won nineteen games and had an ERA of 2.13. Rube Marquard, on the other hand, went from being a nineteen game winner in 1917 to an eighteen game loser in 1918. He won only nine.

Zack Wheat, at age thirty-two, was a bright spot. He feasted on the available arms left in the league and won batting honors with a .335 average. Only eighteen of his 137 hits were for extra bases. He will forever more be remembered by trivia buffs as the last national League player ever to win a batting crown without hitting a single home run.

Jake Daubert was still productive at age thirty-four. He batted .308 and led the league in triples with fifteen. Some of his teammates, due to the shortage of quality players left to compete, were less valuable to say the least.

For example, to fill a gap, Brooklyn had acquired a thirty-eight year old second baseman named Mickey "Doolittle" Dolan. Dolan retired after the season with the dubious distinction of having the lowest career batting average ever for a player with 5,000 or more at bats – .232. He contributed to that distinction by batting .218 in 1918 against highly suspect pitching staffs.

A final note: In this era, before batters learned to step out of the batter's box with impunity, the Giants beat the Dodgers, 1-0, on August 30, 1918, in fifty-seven minutes! Umpires were less patient and would call a pitch a strike, whether the hitter was in the batter's box or not! When we hear all of the calls to speed up Major League baseball game, it might be helpful to remember this simple expedient.

Dodgers		1918	Giants	
Zack Wheat	.335*	**BA**	Ross Youngs	.302
" "	51	**RBI**	Heinie Zimmerman	56
Hy Myers	4	**HR**	George Burns	4
Burleigh Grimes	19	**WINS**	Pol Perritt	18
" " "	2.13	**ERA**	Slim Sallee	2.25
" " "	113	**SO**	Pol Perritt	60

* led the National League

1919

Scandal on the Diamond

1919 was the year that baseball would love to forget. Players had been involved with gamblers since the mid-nineteenth century, and gambling related scandals were common. However, this one could not be overlooked. When it was discovered that eight members of the Chicago White Sox had intentionally thrown the World Series, after another shortened season (140 games) designed to show baseball's support of the war effort, the sport was rocked to its foundations.

The regular season went along normally enough. Babe Ruth hit a Major League record 29 home runs, in addition to pitching twelve complete games, and Ty Cobb won his last batting crown with a .380 batting average.

The Giants finished second again, despite having the league's best offense (605 runs scored). Their batters led in a number of individual statistics: George Burns was tops in runs, 86, walks, 82 and stolen bases, 40; and Ross Youngs led in doubles with 31. Youngs had a ten-year lifetime batting average of .322, before his career was tragically cut short by Bright's disease. He died at age thirty, after the 1927 season.

Two unique events occurred for the Giants. In a September game with the Phillies, they beat their 57-minute defeat of Brooklyn the previous year by dispatching the Phillies in a record, 51 minutes, by a score of 6-1. On a negative note, catcher Mike Gonzalez managed to set a record by allowing eight stolen bases in one inning, on July 7th. Still, the Giants finished second again while the Dodgers languished in fifth-place.

The Giants scored eighty more runs and had a slugging average that was 26 points higher than Brooklyn's but, basically, the teams were fairly close in their statistical achievements. The Dodgers pitchers gave up 103 more hits, but completed 98 games to the Giants 72.

The Giants won eighteen more games than did Brooklyn and drove in 53 more runs. Still, their team batting average was only .06 higher and Dodgers pitchers struck out 176 more batters than did the Giants staff. Dodgers pitchers also walked 23 less. McGraw used nineteen pitchers before the shortened season ended; Wilbert Robinson got by with nine.

For the Giants, Jesse Barnes, out of Perkins, Oklahoma, led the league with 25 wins, while Jeff Pfeffer also came back from the war to once again lead the Dodgers staff with 17 wins. The stability of the that staff (four hurlers won in double figures) should have warned the rest of the league that they would be a factor in 1920.

Brooklyn did have two highlights in 1919. Their first-baseman, "Big Ed" Konetchy from La Crosse, Wisconsin, set a National League record with ten consecutive hits and Hy Myers, the pride of East Liverpool, Ohio, led the league with a .436 slugging average. (It was the lowest slugging average ever to take the title in the history of the National League.)

Dodgers		1919	Giants	
Hy Myers	.307	**BA**	Ross Youngs	.311
" "	73*	**RBI**	Benny Kauff	67
Tommy Griffith	6	**HR**	" "	10
Jeff Pfeffer	17	**WINS**	Jesse Barnes	25*
Sherry Smith	2.24	**ERA**	Fred Toney	1.84
Leon Cadore	94	**SO**	Jesse Barnes	92

* led the National League

1920

Judge Landis Takes Over

1920 was probably the most nerve-wracking, disruptive, saddest year in the history of baseball for everyone but Dodgers fans. Rumors of a gambling fix in the 1919 World Series colored the entire season, and courtroom evidence led many to feel that no baseball results were to be taken seriously. Were the bookmakers controlling the game?

By September, the scandal was no longer in dispute. After months of "honest" and "dishonest" White Sox players operating out of a dissension-plagued clubhouse, yet managing to stay in the thick of the pennant race, the ax fell. Baseball had its first commissioner: an ex-federal judge named Kenesaw Mountain Landis – even the name bespoke rock-hard honesty – with wide discretionary powers. (No commissioner after him would have so much power, but the owners were desperate to save the game.) Landis banned the White Sox stars that were implicated by a grand jury, with two weeks left in the season. Even so, Chicago finished only three games out of first place!

Gambling was not restricted to current White Sox players. "Prince Hal" Chase, a former Yankee and White Sox player, who had been the Giants first baseman in 1919, was discovered to be the go-between. As determined earlier, Heinie Zimmerman and Lee Magee had already been banned from baseball after the 1919 season. (Zimmerman, of course, had played for the Giants; Magee was with the Cubs.)

To make matters worse for baseball's image, Ray Chapman, Cleveland's outstanding shortstop was beaned by the Yankees new ace, Carl Mays. Chapman died only months before he was to wed an heiress of the Gimbel's Department Store family. It was the first and only baseball fatality ever and eventually led to the requirement of batting helmets in professional baseball.

Just as the cries were going up to outlaw organized baseball, along came babe Ruth to save it. For $125,000, that the Red Sox badly needed, he had just been traded to the Yankees with their enticingly short, right-field fence. (The Yankees were still playing their games at the Polo Grounds.) Ruth took full advantage of this delightful situation by belting an astounding (for the time) 54 home runs. With the exception of the last-place Phillies, who hit 64, this was more home runs than any team in both leagues hit in 1920! He was also assisted by a livelier baseball and a few rule changes, such as the elimination of trick pitches like the spitball. (Current practitioners were exempt from the rule.) We can also thank the Babe for years of watching clean baseballs being brought into play and pitchers being warned for even touching their mouths.

The fans loved the new power game. They flocked to see Ruth wherever he appeared and this enthusiasm helped them to forget the dreadful betting scandal and the tragedy of Ray Chapman's untimely death.

What helped the Dodgers and Giants fans to forget the scandal and Chapman's misfortune was the thrill of watching their two teams battle for the National League pennant. It was high drama at Ebbets Field and the Polo Grounds whenever the two teams met. Wilbert Robinson matching wits with John McGraw might have seemed like a mismatch to many, but Wilbert and his boys prevailed.

Brooklyn's spitballer, Burleigh Grimes, led them to the pennant with 23 wins and a 2.22 ERA. The pitching staff led the league with an ERA of 2.62. (The Giants recorded an ERA of 2.80.) The Brooklyn pitching staff had great balance – six different hurlers won ten games or more. The Giants had three 20-game winners: Toney, Nehf and Barnes, and Phil Douglas chipped in fourteen more, but the other nine members of the staff contributed a total of only ten wins. The Giants led the league in shutouts with eighteen, but the Dodgers fireballers had 553 strikeouts to the Giants 380.

At the plate, the Giants got a league-leading 94 RBI's from first-baseman, George "High-pockets" Kelly, who also led the league in striking out – he did so 92 times. At 6'4" George's nickname came naturally. Their two veterans, Larry Doyle and George Burns also had productive years and Ross Youngs, who had broken in with a .311 batting average in 1919, soared to .351. Doyle retired at the end of the year with the dubious honor of holding the record for most career errors by a second baseman, 443. Youngs finished second to Rogers Hornsby, who won the batting crown with a .370.

Brooklyn had three .300 hitters, with Zack Wheat leading the club at .328. Burleigh Grimes showed that he could hit as well as pitch. While he was no Babe Ruth, Grimes did produce 34 hits in 111 at-bats for a very respectable .306 batting average.

None of this helped in the World Series as the Dodgers flopped again. Cleveland romped, five games to two, in a series that featured a few firsts: an unassisted triple play by Cleveland's second-baseman, Bill Wambsganss, a home run by a pitcher (Cleveland's Jim Bagby) and the first World Series grand slam home run, also by an Indian, Elmer Smith. In another interesting sidelight to the event, the Series saw brothers on opposing teams. Doc Johnston was the Indian first baseman and brother Jimmy (known as "Dirty Jack") was the Dodgers third-sacker. They both got three hits.

After the first two decades of the twentieth century had passed, the Giants could look back at a clear advantage over their cross-town rivals. The Giants had won six pennants, the Dodgers only three. They had outscored the Dodgers by more than two thousand runs (12,901 to 10,816), had a team batting average twelve points higher (.263-.251) and had hit 103 more home runs (585 to 482).

Their pitchers ERA's for the two decades were lower than the Dodgers (2.65-2.93); they had struck out 1270 more batters and had thirty more shutouts.

The Dodgers finished in the first division only five times in those twenty years, the Giants were only out of the first division three times. In addition, the Giants had put together four 100-win seasons during this period; the Dodgers would not reach the 100-win plateau until 1941. Ironically, the Giants would never post another 100-win season in the Polo Grounds after their 101 victories in 1913.

With the Giants destined to win the pennant four consecutive times, beginning in 1921, the gap between the two team's accomplishments could only widen.

Dodgers		**1920**	**Giants**	
Zack Wheat	.328	**BA**	Ross Youngs	.351
Hy Myers	80	**RBI**	George Kelly	94*
Zack Wheat	9	**HR**	" "	11
Burleigh Grimes	23	**WINS**	Art Nehf Fred Toney	21
" " "	2.22	**ERA**	Jesse Barnes Fred Toney	2.65
" " "	131	**SO**	Fred Toney	81

* led the National League

1921

McGraw Makeover Spells Pennant

John McGraw gained his revenge on those who saw his three consecutive second-place finishes as proof that he was losing his touch. His remaking of the Giants led to a pennant and, as icing on the cake, a World Series victory over the favored Yankees. It was his seventh pennant in nineteen years and was the first of four consecutive flags that his Giants were to win at the onset of the "Roaring Twenties."

Better pitching in the World Series was the Giants main weapon. Ruth was held to one home run, although a bad arm kept him out of the last three games, and the Giants ERA was 2.53, as compared to the Yankees 3.09. It was the first ever "Subway Series" and the New York fans loved it. It was also the last time that a World Series would be decided in a best-of-nine-game format.

Most of the interest in the series centered upon the Babe, who had put together what was possibly the best statistical year in baseball history. The Bambino hit 59 home runs, had 204 hits, drove in 171 runs, batted .378 and had an unbelievable slugging average of .846! Most players would consider any one of the above accomplishments enough to call it a successful year. Ruth accomplished all of the above despite receiving a league-leading 144 walks. He also was called upon to pitch nine innings, and got credit for two wins despite a 9.00 ERA.

During the season, the Giants were led by George Kelly, who hit 23 home runs, to top the National League in that department, and drove in 122 runs, while batting .308. Frisch (.341), Youngs (.327), Meusel (.329), Snyder (.320) and Bancroft (.318) all had banner years. The Giants needed all of it to win over a tough Pittsburgh team, whose pitching kept them in the race until late August. At that point, the Giants swept a five-game series with them to pull away for good.

The Giants team batting average was .298 and, if George Burns had hit one point higher, the Giants would have had seven regulars batting over .300 in the same season! (Incidentally, Burns holds the National League record for steals of home – 26.) Clearly, the lively ball had taken over. Cincinnati had the *lowest* batting average in the National League, with a .278 and the Cardinals, as a team, were actually above .300 at .308!

The Dodgers, meanwhile, after their unexpected 1920 pennant, slumped badly to a 77-75 record and a fifth-place finish. Burleigh Grimes won 22 games, and the workhorse hurler led the league with thirty complete games and 136 strikeouts. Unfortunately, the rest of the staff sagged. Jeff Pfeffer, a sixteen-game winner the previous year, came up with a dead arm, at age 33, and finished with a dismal 1-5 record. Leon Cadore went from 15-14 in 1920 to 13-14 in 1921. His ERA soared from 2.62 to 4.16.

Better pitching might have kept the Dodgers in the chase. They had four regulars hitting above .300 including, "Old Reliable" Zack Wheat at .320, but the Dodgers were aging badly. Six of their eight regulars were over thirty, as were three of their top five pitchers.

To compare the two clubs, the Giants tallied 840 runs to the Dodgers 667. The Giants team batting average was eighteen points higher, and they hit sixteen more home runs. They got 99 more hits and their pitchers gave up 59 less than did the Brooklyn staff. Perhaps the most telling statistic was the average age of the teams. The Giants were at 27, while the Dodgers had an average age of 31. Tired legs do not win close ball games in the late innings.

1921 was the year that the first baseball game was broadcast. It happened in Pittsburgh on August 25th. Also, that year, a pioneer opened a door in the Major Leagues for others to follow. Specs Toporcer, a utility infielder for the Cardinals, became the first Major Leaguer, other than a pitcher, to wear glasses on the field. (The nickname is obvious; his real name was George.)

Dodgers		1921	Giants	
Jimmy Johnston	.325	BA	Frankie Frisch	.341
Zack Wheat	85	RBI	George Kelly	122
" "	14	HR	" "	23*
Burleigh Grimes	22*	WINS	Art Nehf	20
" " "	2.84	ERA	Jesse Barnes	3.10
" " "	136*	SO	Art Nehf	67

* led the National League

1922

Giants Win Again

The Giants did it again in 1922, finishing seven games ahead of Cincinnati and seventeen games ahead of sixth-place Brooklyn. Thirty-one-year-old Casey Stengel, in his second year with the Giants, hit .368 in seventy-seven games. The left-handed hitter from Kansas City, Missouri was improving with age. The only starter on this Giants juggernaut to hit under .321 (Dave Bancroft's batting average) was third baseman, Heinie Groh, who ended the season at .265. He would, however, find glory in the World Series.

The team batting average was a hefty .304, second in the national League only to third place Pittsburgh, which posted a .308. The big Giants bats made up for a pitching staff that, for the first time ever on a pennant winner, lacked a twenty-game winner. They did, however, lead the league in ERA with a 3.45, and Rosy Ryan was best in the league with a 3.00 ERA.

Jesse Barnes, out of Perkins, Oklahoma, provided a pitching highlight when he threw a no-hitter against the Phillies for one of his thirteen wins. The Giants ace, Phil Douglas, the pride of Cedartown, Georgia, might have made it to twenty wins but, when he reached eleven, he wrote an idiotic letter that, unfortunately, became public. In it, he implied that he would welcome bribes to throw games. He was suspended and "Shufflin' Phil," as he was called was finished in baseball at the age of thirty-two. Despite this early, and final, curtailment of his activities, Douglas was still the only pitcher in the National League to throw for 150 innings or more and have an ERA under 3.00.

The Dodgers, with only three regulars under the age of thirty-two, finished below .500 and in sixth place. They were 76-78 on the season. Five regulars managed to connect enough times with the "jackrabbit" ball that was inflating pitchers ERA's to hit over .300, and with a twenty-game winner in Dutch Reuther (21-12), they lacked only one thing – consistency. Only three of their hurlers (Reuther, Vance and Grimes) won more than eight games and the staff had the further "distinction" of leading the league in both bases on balls (490) and strikeouts (499). Their ERA's were also unimpressive: Reuther had the lowest (3.54); Vance was at 3.70 and Grimes suffered an inflated 4.75. Dazzy Vance, from Orient, Iowa, did lead the league with 134 strikeouts, although it was a record for the lowest total ever to take that particular honor.

Zack Wheat took all of the batting titles for the club. He hit .335, knocked in 112 runs and had sixteen home runs. Quite a contrast from 1918, when he won the batting crown without hitting a single homer. Jimmy Johnston, a utility infielder out of Cleveland, Tennessee, hit .319; Griffith, Myers and DeBerry also reached the .300 plateau.

The Giants star shone brightly in the World Series. McGraw watched gleefully as his troops swept the Yankees in four games for a second consecutive win over Ruth and company. Ruth was a dismal two for seventeen (a .118 batting average) with no home runs. In contrast, Groh, the Giants weakest hitter during the regular season, led all hitters with a .474. Scrappy Frankie Frisch was right behind him with eight hits in seventeen at-bats for a .471 mark.

1922 was clearly a hitter's year. Rogers Hornsby became the first undisputed Triple Crown winner in National League history. He not only hit .401, but led the league with forty-two homers and 152 RBI's. His slugging average was an impressive .722 to lead all others, and he was first in runs scored with 141 and doubles (46). When you add fourteen triples and seventeen stolen bases to the above, it seems clear as to why the Cardinals could tie with Pittsburgh for third place, only one game behind second-place

Cincinnati. Hornsby was a one-man gang. He also led all National League second basemen in putouts, double plays and fielding percentage. Is it any wonder that McGraw made up his mind that someday Hornsby would be a Giant?

Dodgers		**1922**	**Giants**	
Zack Wheat	.335	**BA**	Casey Stengel	.368
" "	112	**RBI**	Irish Meusel	132
" "	16	**HR**	George Kelly	17
Dutch Ruether	21	**WINS**	Art Nehf	19
" " "	3.54	**ERA**	Rosy Ryan	3.00*
Dazzy Vance	134*	**SO**	" "	75

* led the National League

81

The heart of the Giants dynasty *(left to right):* George Kelly, Travis Jackson, Freddie Maguire, Frankie Frisch, Dave Bancroft and Heinie Groh at the start of the 1923 campaign.

1923

The Babe Triumphs in World Series

In 1922, Whitey Witt, one of the Yankees "other" outfielders, who hit four home runs all year, got more bases-on-balls than did Babe Ruth – he got eighty-nine to Ruth's eighty-four. Pitchers were smarter in 1923; the Babe walked 170 times. He still managed to hit forty-one home runs to lead the American League. Surprisingly, an outfielder for the Phillies named Cy Williams hit that many to lead the National League! Williams hit a total of 251 four-baggers in a nineteen year career, and could always brag that he hit as many as the Babe in 1923 when they both led their leagues.

In what must have sent waves of depression through all of the other Major League cities, New York once again boasted both entries in the World Series for the third straight year. The 1922 World Series had been played at the Polo Grounds since that was still the home field for both clubs. However, possibly due to resentment of Ruth's and the Yankees popularity, the Giants informed the Yankees during the off-season that they were no longer welcome as tenants. (The fact that the Yankees consistently outdrew the Giants finally became too much for Giants management to bear.)

Thus prodded, Colonel Jacob Ruppert, the Yankees owner, responded by erecting Yankee Stadium – ever after known as the "House that Ruth built." The Stadium was built in an amazing 284 days. The Yankees celebrated by winning the pennant and the World Series in their new surroundings. It was their first ever World Championship.

The Yankees won the Series, four games to two as Ruth, who had been stifled the year before, hit three home runs and batted .368. The future Yankees managerial genius, Casey Stengel, used all year as an alternate center fielder by McGraw, had two home runs and batted .417 in the Series. In fact, Stengel won the first game of the Fall Classic with an inside-the-park home run and his homer in the third game accounted for the Giants run in a 1-0 victory. However, those were the only games won by the Giants; Stengel's heroics became in vain as the Yankees then swept the next three games. It might have been those exploits that led Casey to reminisce in later years: "I was such a dangerous hitter, that I got intentional walks in batting practice."

It was an unpleasant ending to what had been a great year for the Giants. They won ninety-five games and thrilled their fans by winning a close race with the Reds in a newly refurbished Polo Grounds. (It had been expanded to seat 54,000.) Once again lacking a twenty-game winner, the Giants relied on five hurlers who all won in double figures.

McGraw revealed yet another managerial talent as he proved to be a master in the judicious use of relief pitchers. The Giants led the league with eighteen saves. (By comparison, Brooklyn had five saves for the year.) The Giants Claude Jonnard, from Nashville, Tennessee, may have quietly made history as baseball's first consistently successful relief pitcher (although many "experts" give that title to Firpo Marberry of the American League Washington Senators, because of his fifteen saves in 1925). Still, this writer feels that Jonnard should get the credit for appearing in a league-leading forty-five games for the second straight year, and for garnering five saves. (He retired with seventeen saves to his credit.)

Frankie Frisch had a great year to go with his World Series success. The "Fordham Flash" batted .348, led the league in hits with 223, scored 116 runs, knocked in 111 and even had twelve home runs. Frisch added twenty-nine stolen bases and led the team in slugging percentage with a .485. Frisch's bat control was truly amazing: he played in all 152 games, yet struck out only twelve times in 641 at-bats!

The Giants led the National League with 854 runs scored. Ross Youngs, the pride of Shriner, Texas, had another good year, batting .336 and leading the league with 121 runs scored. Bob (Irish) Meusel, actually, Emil, from Oakland, California, also led the National League with 125 RBI's (He had eight more in the World Series) to complete the Giants dominance of offensive categories. The Giants even set a twentieth century record by scoring at least one run in every inning against Philadelphia on June 1st. The feat would not be duplicated until 1964 by St. Louis against the Cubs. (Twenty-five years later, the Colorado Rockies did it to the Cubs again.) No American League team has ever done it in this century.

Even the Giants pitchers could hit. Jack Bentley, in addition to leading the staff in strikeouts with eighty and winning thirteen games, set a league record for pitchers by batting .427 in eighty-nine at-bats. This performance naturally led to cries that the next Babe Ruth had arrived; however, Bentley did not quite fulfill that prediction. He won forty-six games and lost thirty-four in a career that ended, ironically, in 1927, when the Babe hit sixty home runs. The six-foot tall, lefthander, out of Sandy Spring, Maryland, retired with a very respectable lifetime .291 batting average, but only seven homers in 584 at-bats.

The Dodgers, like the rest of the National League, could only look on enviously as the Giants dynasty continued. They were sixth again, with exactly the same won-lost record, 76-78 that they had compiled the previous year.

Once again, their pitching was good – they led the league in strikeouts (548) and complete games (94). Burleigh Grimes won twenty-one games and Vance and Reuther won eighteen and fifteen respectively. However, none of the other hurlers on the club were effective. In fact, these three accounted for seventy-four of the ninety-four complete games posted by the staff. Unlike McGraw, Robinson rarely used relief pitchers. Art Decauter led the team with three saves.

Jack Fournier, a thirty-year-old first baseman, out of Au Sable, Michigan, traded to Brooklyn by St. Louis, had a great year. Fournier batted .351 and belted twenty-two home runs. (More than one-third of the entire team's total of sixty-two.) Unfortunately, Jimmy Johnston was the only other .300 hitter on the club. The Dodgers sorely missed Zack Wheat, who was hitting .375 after eighty-seven games, but was injured and missed the rest of the season.

Rookie Moe Berg, later to become known for his involvement as an early "agent 007" for our government, played forty-seven games at shortstop and batted an anemic .186. (He may have been personally responsible for the coining of the baseball description: "Good field, no hit!")

Berg's intelligence and a career change to catcher enabled him to spend sixteen years in the Major Leagues despite a lifetime batting average of only .243. A number of star pitchers loved the way he handled them and insisted upon Moe when they were on the mound.

Dodgers	1923		Giants	
Jack Fournier	.351	**BA**	Frankie Frisch	.348
" " "	102	**RBI**	Irish Meusel	125*
" " "	22	**HR**	" "	19
Burleigh Grimes	21	**WINS**	Rosy Ryan Jack Scott	16
Dazzy Vance	3.50	**ERA**	Hugh McQuillen	3.40
" "	197*	**SO**	Jack Bentley	80

* led the National League

1924

Giants Lose Again in World Series

1924 was another carbon copy of a year for the Giants. They captured a fourth consecutive pennant despite not having any pitcher on the staff who would win more than sixteen games. In addition, the team ERA was a hefty 3.62. Clearly, their bats had once again brought them the flag. The team had a .300 batting average, with Ross Youngs leading the way at .355.

Four other Giants hit over .300 as they led the league in team batting average; team slugging average; RBI's; home runs; runs scored and hits. George Kelly set a record with seven home runs in six consecutive games (later to be tied by two other Giants – Walker Cooper and Willie Mays).

The game had changed and McGraw had changed with it. Ruth's heroics had made offense and the long ball dominant over the bunt, the stolen base, and the hit and run. As an indication of how much the game had changed, the Giants, who had stolen 347 bases in 1911, led the National League in 1924 with ninety-five! With the juiced up ball now flying out of the park more regularly, stealing bases had become much more of a risk.

The Giants competition in 1924 came from an unexpected source: the Dodgers rebounded from a dismal sixth place finish in 1923 to challenge for the pennant all the way to the wire. They fell short by only 1½ games.

It was the Brooklyn pitching staff that kept them in the hunt. At age thirty-three, Dazzy Vance led the league in strikeouts with 262 and in ERA, 2.16. He won twenty-eight games and lost only six! Burleigh Grimes added twenty-two wins and 135 strikeouts. The Dodgers staff led the league with 638 strikeouts – 232 more than the Giants and 274 more than the third place Pirates.

The Dodgers had some offense too. Jack Fournier led the league in home runs with twenty-seven and Zack Wheat, at age thirty-eight, hit .375 in 141 games. Wheat rapped out 212 hits (only the great Rogers Hornsby had more) and even belted fourteen homers. Speaking of Hornsby, this was the year that he set a standard that holds to the present day. He batted .424, with 227 hits, a slugging average of .696 and the scoring of 121 runs. All of this for a sixth place Cardinals team that won only sixty-five games!

In a bittersweet moment for Brooklyn's manager, Wilbert Robinson, he was forced to watch Jim Bottomley of the Cardinals drive in twelve runs against his club on September 6th. It broke the record of eleven RBI's in a single game that Wilbert had set as an active player with the Baltimore Orioles in the previous century.

On a tragic note, Jake Daubert, who had starred for Brooklyn from 1910 to 1918, died after a routine operation. He was only forty.

Even more surprising than the Dodgers surge to the top, was the fact that the fourth straight subway series between the Giants and the Yankees, that everyone had taken for granted, did not materialize. The Yankees were shocked by a Washington club that had finished fourth in 1923. Walter Johnson proved the difference with a league-leading twenty-three wins and a 2.72 ERA. It was the eighteenth consecutive year of brilliance for the thirty-six year old right-hander and, with the exception of Yankees fans, everyone was happy to see him finally make it to the World Series.

It looked like the Series itself would be anticlimactic for Johnson. The Giants beat him in his first two starts. However, fate decreed that he would have one more chance as Washington and New York battled to a seventh and deciding game. In the eighth inning of that game, Johnson came in to relieve and held the Giants scoreless until the twelfth, when Washington scored to take the championship and make Johnson a Series winner at last.

While Johnson now had his treasured World Series victory, John McGraw was left with the dubious distinction of having lost more World Series games (28) than any other manager in baseball history. This may have rankled McGraw, but it certainly could in no way tarnish his achievements as a manager.

Dodgers		1924	Giants	
Zack Wheat	.375	**BA**	Ross Youngs	.355
Jack Fournier	116	**RBI**	George Kelly	136*
" "	27*	**HR**	" " "	21
Dazzy Vance	28*	**WINS**	Virgil Barnes	16
			Jack Bentley	
" "	2.16*	**ERA**	Hugh McQuillen	2.69
" "	262*	**SO**	Art Nehf	72

* led the National League

89

1925

Bill Terry Makes his Mark

Hornsby wasn't bad in 1925 either. The Winters, Texas icon won his sixth straight National League batting title, captured the Triple Crown, was named the National League's Most Valuable Player, batted .403, hit thirty-nine home runs and knocked in 143. As if that wasn't enough for any mere mortal, he replaced Branch Rickey (of future Brooklyn front office fame) as manager and moved the Cardinals up from sixth in 1924 to fourth place.

Despite high expectations, the Giants did not win their fifth consecutive pennant. They came in second to a young, solid Pittsburgh club that had a team batting average of .307. The Pirates were also the first National League team to ever score 900 runs in a single season – they tallied 912.

In his third year as a Giant, Bill Terry took possession of first base and, the left-handed hitting, future Hall-of-Famer, hit .319 in 133 games. (McGraw was a hard man to impress though. Terry became a benchwarmer again the following season as McGraw named George Kelly as his first baseman.)

The Giants might have overtaken the Pirates if they had not been so hampered by injuries. Ross Youngs' infected kidneys had him slumping to a .264 batting average. Frisch was hobbled by an ankle injury – although he still managed to play in 120 games and bat .331. Irish Meusel led the club with a .328 batting average, 111 RBI's and twenty-one home runs. (Kelly had twenty.) Most detrimental to the team's offense was the unexpected failure of Hack Wilson, who had hit a respectable .295 the year before. Hack slumped so badly that McGraw sent him to Toledo after sixty-two games. (That move would have repercussions later.)

Most serious for the club was their continued lack of a twenty-game winner. Once again, they relied on a number of starters and it almost worked as six of them won in double figures. The defect was made more poignant by news that their former ace, Christy Mathewson, had died at the age of forty-five. He never fully recovered from his gassing at the front in 1918 and had succumbed to tuberculosis.

Dazzy Vance was the bright spot for a Dodgers team that slumped back to sixth place. (They were to remain mired in sixth-place for the next four seasons!) Vance, out of Orient, Iowa, struck out 221 batters in a year when only four other pitchers – in *both* leagues – struck out one hundred or more. Vance won twenty-two games for a team that recorded a total of only sixty-eight victories.

Obviously, it was another year of the lively ball. Major League batters set a record by hitting the "rabbit" ball for a composite .292 batting average. With a team batting average of .296, the Dodgers did not even lead the league – in fact, they were third! The Giants, while finishing four spots above them in the standings, hit at a .283 clip.

Brooklyn's problem was that, after Vance, Grimes with twelve wins and Ehrhardt with ten were the only pitchers on the team with double digit victories – and both of them lost more games than they won. In fact, Grimes led the league in losses with nineteen. (His 5.03 ERA helps to explain those losses.) Ehrhardt was no better, managing to lose fourteen games by virtue of a 5.02 ERA. They both walked more batters than they struck out. By comparison, Vance walked only sixty-six to go with his 221 strikeouts. Vance also had all four of the staff's shutouts.

Zack Wheat led Brooklyn's hitters with a .359 average and Fournier hit .350. (Wheat had turned thirty-nine that May, but obviously could still swing the bat.) The sixth-place Dodgers actually outscored the second-place Giants by almost fifty runs (786 - 737) and their team batting average was higher (.296 - .283). The difference was in the pitching. The Giants ERA of 3.94 bested the Brooklyn ERA of 4.77, and Giants pitchers walked sixty-nine less batters. The importance of good pitching is exemplified by the disparity between the two clubs in the standings for 1925.

Dodgers		1925	Giants	
Zack Wheat	.359	**BA**	Frankie Frisch	.331
Jack Fournier	130	**RBI**	Irish Meusel	111
" "	22	**HR**	" "	21
Dazzy Vance	22	**WINS**	Virgil Barnes	15
" "	3.53	**ERA**	Jack Scott	3.15
" "	221*	**SO**	" '	87

* led the National League

1926

"Master Melvin" Arrives

In 1926, Rogers Hornsby, now in his first full year as manager, led the Cardinals to their first pennant of the twentieth Century and a World Series win over a heavily favored Yankees club. They did so despite Babe Ruth's breaking of two World Series records – three home runs in one game and four homers in a Series.

In addition to his full-time managing, Hornsby batted .317 and drove in ninety-three runs. His reward for this achievement? The "grateful" Cardinals traded him that December to the Giants for Frankie Frisch and a thirty-one year old pitcher named Jimmie Ring. (Ring never won a game for the Cardinals, but it didn't matter – Frisch was the key player in the deal.)

Meanwhile, the Giants fell to fifth place in 1926 and McGraw felt that he had to have Hornsby's bat at any price. When it became clear that he could only get Hornsby by trading Frisch, McGraw made the trade at the end of the season. At first, it looked like McGraw had outsmarted everyone again. The Cardinals, in 1927, dropped to second place, while the Giants, with Hornsby, rose two spots to third. In time, though, the Cardinals more than got the better of the deal.

Travis Jackson led the Giants in 1926 with a .327 batting average. George Kelly led the club in home runs with thirteen but Irish Meusel, who had led the club in 1925 with twenty-one homers, hit only six in 112 games. Although, he was only thirty-one, Meusel appeared to be washed up. He was traded to the Dodgers at the end of the season – appeared in forty-two games for them, with one home run and was finished as a Major Leaguer. There is not much sentiment in baseball for players whose skills erode. (Babe Ruth being traded to the Braves at the end of his career is, of course, the best known example.)

In a season of streaks, the Giants managed to set two records. They won twenty-six consecutive home games and seventeen consecutive road games. However, their perennial lack of a twenty-game winner hurt them again – this time resulting in a second division finish for the first time since 1915. Freddie Fitzsimmons, out of the metropolis of Mishawaka, Indiana, disproved the so-called "sophomore jinx" by leading the Giants with fourteen wins and a 2.88 ERA. Frisch, in his last year with the club, and the always-reliable Ross Youngs hit over .300 but the team was inconsistent.

Ross Youngs was taken ill after ninety-five games. Sadly, he died in October of the following year, cutting short a brilliant career that ended much too soon for him at the age of only twenty-nine. He had a career batting average of .322 and most pundits felt that he was McGraw's favorite player.

It was a bitter loss for the team but, as so often happens in baseball (witness Wally Pipp's injury that allowed Lou Gehrig to get his opportunity), Youngs' tragic illness opened the door for a seventeen-year-old, left-handed batter to play ten games in the outfield and to do some pinch-hitting against the tougher right-handed pitchers. In sixty at-bats, the youngster opened some eyes by hitting .383. Mel Ott, from Gretna, Louisiana, had arrived at the Polo Grounds. That year, he became the youngest player in National League history to get a pinch hit. He would add a few more records in the course of his long and illustrious career.

The Dodgers once again landed in sixth place, four games behind the Giants, with a record of 71-82 for the year. Despite their poor season, the Dodgers entertained their fans with the debut of a crowd-pleasing, left-handed first baseman named Babe Herman.

The twenty-three-year-old, from Buffalo, New York, was atrocious in the field. (He was finally converted to a full-time right-fielder in 1928, where he made fewer, though more glaring, errors.) However, he could hit, and for power. In his rookie year, Herman led the club with eighty-one RBI's and tied for the club lead in home runs with Jack Fournier by clouting eleven. He was Brooklyn's only .300 hitter (.319) and his slugging average of .500 was second highest in the National League. (Cy Williams, of the Phillies, took the honor with a slugging average of .568.) An impressive fifty-seven of Herman's 158 hits were for extra bases. As might be expected of a power hitter, he also led the club in strikeouts with fifty-three.

At age forty, Zack Wheat played in 102 games and hit a respectable .290. As for the pitching staff, Burleigh Grimes slipped to a 12-13 mark, but Jesse Petty, from Orr, Oklahoma, stepped up to lead the team with seventeen wins. (Unfortunately, he lost an equal amount.) Petty's fast ball kept batters on their heels, but the lack of control that kept hitters edgy led to Petty's career totals showing more losses than wins. Dazzy Vance, at age thirty-five managed only nine wins, but he still had enough to lead the National League with 140 strikeouts. Age continued to be a problem for the Dodgers staff. Of eight regular pitchers, seven were thirty or older, and the "youngest" was twenty-nine. Clearly, some fresh new arms were sorely needed.

Dodgers		1926	Giants	
Babe Herman	.319	**BA**	Travis Jackson	.327
" "	81	**RBI**	George Kelly	80
Jack Fournier Babe Herman	11	**HR**	" "	13
Jesse Petty	17	**WINS**	Freddie Fitzsimmons	14
" "	2.84	**ERA**	Virgil Barnes	2.87
Dazzy Vance	140*	**SO**	Jack Scott	82

* led the National League

Spring Training at Sarasota, Florida, 1927. McGraw poses with three of this year's stars *(left to right)*: Burleigh Grimes, Rogers Hornsby and Edd Roush. Five years later, McGraw would retire.

1927

The Year of Hornsby

Mention 1927 and fans immediately think of Babe Ruth and his sixty home runs. Most will not recall that it was Ruth's teammate, Lou Gehrig, who was the American League's Most Valuable Player that year. In addition, there *were* pennant races in both leagues.

The Giants, with Rogers Hornsby playing second base and hitting .361, moved up to third place and finished the season only two games behind first place Pittsburgh. Bill Terry hit .326 as a full-time first baseman, Travis Jackson, the shortstop, hit .318 and Fred Lindstrom, at the hot corner hit .306 to complete a powerhouse infield. With his usual sagacity as a trader, McGraw had picked up a little known thirty-five-year-old outfielder from the Phillies named George Harper. All that he did was to deliver a .331 batting average and hit sixteen home runs. The veteran outfielder also drew eighty-four walks – only two less than the league leader, Rogers Hornsby.

With all of this offense, the Giants might have won it all if not for an unfortunate error by the front office. You may recall that McGraw had sent Hack Wilson to Toledo in 1925, when Wilson slumped at the plate. Unfortunately, the club secretary, Jim Tierney, had neglected to put Wilson back on the Giants roster. The Cubs took advantage of the omission and grabbed Wilson. It was a good move. Hack hit .318 for Chicago and led the league with thirty home runs.

The Giants pitching staff had not featured a twenty-game winner since Art Nehf accomplished the feat in 1921, and this year was no exception. Burleigh Grimes, picked up from the Dodgers, came close at 19-8, and Fitzsimmons was 17-10. Virgil Barnes, from Ontario, Kansas, garnered fourteen wins behind the Giants big bats and, in an oddity, Virgil started a game against his brother, Jesse, of the Braves on May 3rd. It marked the first time that brothers had ever started a Major League game against each other. Virgil won.

Another Giants hurler, Larry Benton, "stolen" from the Braves in midseason in another of McGraw's shrewd moves, won nine games for them and ended the season with a 17-7 record – a .708 winning percentage that led the National League. Once again, McGraw's enlightened use of relief pitchers helped the Giants to lead the league in saves with sixteen. By comparison, Joe McCarthy, in his second year as manager of the fourth place Cubs, and only four years away from his glory years as manager of the Yankees, had a staff that recorded a total of five saves for the year. Many of the Giants saves resulted from their big bats "saving" the day. It certainly was not often the pitching staff, which posted a 3.97 ERA, the third worst in the league.

The Dodgers staff recorded a far better ERA (3.36), but their team batting average was only .254, compared to the Giants .297; and the Giants led the National League with a slugging average of .427. With a slugging average of only .342 (less than Rogers Hornsby's *batting* average), the Dodgers hitters gave their pitchers minimal support. Harvey Hendrick was their only .300 hitter. A well traveled Jigger Statz (actually, out of baseball the previous year) was next best with a .274 batting average. Jigger also led the club in striking out, with forty-three whiffs. Max Carey, at the tender age of thirty-seven, led the club in stolen bases with forty-three. Babe Herman had slipped to a .272 batting average, but did slug fourteen home runs. The entire Brooklyn team hit only thirty-nine. After Herman, the next highest home run total on the team was seven, by Jay Partridge. (Jay became a fixture in the Dodgers front office for many years after his brief career – two years – as a utility infielder for the team.)

Manager Wilbert Robinson had seen enough of Herman's ineptitude at first base and moved him to the outfield for the 1928 season. His antics at that position would become the stuff of legend.

The Giants of 1927 scored 817 runs to the Dodgers meager total of 541. They had a team batting average that was forty-four points higher than Brooklyn's and, in general, they were far ahead in every offensive category. The Giants led the league in homers with 109 and RBI's with 765. The Dodgers were far behind with their thirty-nine home runs and 499 RBI's. The Giants also had 280 more hits. Brooklyn did manage to lead in two categories: triples, 74-62 and stolen bases, 106 to 73.

No one could ever quite figure out what made McGraw so successful as a manager, and his treatment of Rogers Hornsby became just another part of the mystery. After pursuing Hornsby for years and finally giving up a young star like Frankie Frisch for him, McGraw traded him at the end of the season for a promising, but untried, young catcher from Boston named Shanty Hogan. Hornsby had just led the National League in walks (86), on-base percentage (.448), slugging average (.586) and had tied for the lead in runs scored with 133, in addition to his .361 batting average – second only to Pittsburgh's Paul Waner (.380).

Could Hornsby's success as a manager at St. Louis have worried McGraw? Perhaps he was not prepared to have his successor waiting on the bench. A more simple explanation may be that the same personality traits of Hornsby's that got him fired after a successful year with St. Louis, grated on McGraw too. After only one year with Boston, the latter part as manager, Horsnby was traded once again – this time to the Cubs. (He hit .380 for them and led them to a pennant.) Hornsby, one of the greatest hitters in baseball history (he had a lifetime BA of .358) never found a permanent home as a player or manager in a career that spanned four decades. There must have been a reason.

Dodgers		1927	Giants	
Harvey Hendrick	.310	**BA**	Rogers Hornsby	.361
Babe Herman	73	**RBI**	" " "	125
" "	14	**HR**	" " "	26
Dazzy Vance	16	**WINS**	Burleigh Grimes	19
" "	2.70	**ERA**	" " "	3.53
" "	184*	**SO**	" " "	102

* led the National League

1928

Carl Hubbell Makes his Debut

While 1928 was pretty much of a repeat for the Dodgers (sixth-place again), the Giants moved up to second with a brilliant September that saw them win twenty-five games in that month. They finished only two games behind St. Louis. (The Pirates had slipped to fourth.) At age thirty, Larry Benton became the ace of the Giants staff with a 25-9 won-lost record and an ERA of 2.73. Fitzsimmons also had a great year, winning twenty, while losing only nine. In addition, a twenty-five-year-old rookie lefthander from Carthage, Missouri had joined the staff and started eighteen games. He went ten and six, pitched a shutout and had a more than respectable ERA of 2.83. He would stick around for a while as he perfected a screwball that would make him famous. Later known as "The Meal Ticket" and "King Carl," he would star for fifteen more years – all with the Giants – and amass 253 wins, pitch thirty-six shutouts, strike out 1,677 batters and finish with an ERA under 3.00. Carl Hubbell had arrived at the Polo Grounds.

Good things do, sometimes, come in pairs. In addition to Hubbell, Mel Ott, now a mature nineteen-year-old, had become a regular. He batted .322, with eighteen home runs.

Fred Lindstrom played 153 games for John McGraw at age thirty-five, and led the club with a .358 batting average and 107 RBI's. His 231 hits, which he duplicated in 1930, not only led the National League, but is still a record for third basemen. Right behind him was Bill Terry, having another solid year with a .326 batting average, seventeen home runs and 101 RBI's.

With Rogers Hornsby traded to the Cubs (and by them to Boston) during the previous winter, the Giants had a new second baseman – Andy Cohen. While no Rogers Hornsby (few were), he hit a respectable .274 with nine home runs and 138 hits in 129 games. In addition, McGraw once again displayed his uncanny ability to squeeze another good year out of a veteran by picking up Lefty O'Doul. The Yankees and Red Sox had tried O'Doul as both a pitcher and an outfielder, but he was a much better hitter than hurler. O'Doul hit .319 for McGraw in 94 games.

Meanwhile, Wilbert Robinson and his cast of misfits and aging veterans kept plodding along in their accustomed sixth-place position. Dazzy Vance, at age thirty-seven, was a bright spot – winning twenty-two games and leading the league in strikeouts with 200. He also had the National League's best ERA, 2.09. It was the sixth consecutive year that Vance had led the senior circuit in strikeouts! While he would not lead the league again, he would lead the club in strikeouts for two more seasons. Babe Herman, now a permanent outfielder, led the club with a .340 batting average. Del Bissonette, a twenty-eight-year old rookie, played every game at first base, hit .320 and led the club with twenty-five homers. Unlike Herman, he could also field!

Left-handed hitting, third baseman Harvey Hendrick had his second consecutive .300 season, hitting .318. He also set a National League record when he became the first player to steal three bases in one inning on June 12th.

Those were the highlights for Brooklyn. Their team batting average, .260, was the lowest in the league. They hit only 66 home runs (The Giants led the league with 118) and with 1,393 hits, they had the lowest total of any team in the league. By comparison, the Giants had 1,600 hits. With Dazzy Vance aging, shortstop Dave Bancroft already thirty-seven and Max Carey at thirty-eight, things looked bleak for Brooklyn's chances in 1929 – and they were.

A special note for "Peanuts" fans. The real Red Baron(n) appeared in ten games for the last-place Braves, got four hits in twenty-one at-bats and was never seen again. (Except, possibly, by Snoopy.)

Dodgers		1928	Giants	
Babe Herman	.340	**BA**	Fred Lindstrom	.358
Del Bissonette	106	**RBI**	" " "	107
" " "	25	**HR**	Mel Ott	18
Dazzy Vance	22	**WINS**	Larry Benton	25*
" "	2.09*	**ERA**	" "	2.73
" "	200*	**SO**	" "	90

* led the National League

1929

Terry and Ott Star, but ...

The Giants slipped to third in 1929, thirteen and-a-half games behind the Cubs, who roared past the Pirates to take the pennant by 10½ games. Bill Terry was once again outstanding for the Giants. He delivered a .372 batting average and a .522 slugging average. Andy Cohen and Travis Jackson, the slick double-play combination, both batted .294 and Jackson belted twenty-one homers.

At age twenty, Mel Ott had learned to take full advantage of the cozy right field porch at the Polo Grounds. He smacked forty-two home runs to become the youngest Major Leaguer to ever hit forty or more home runs in a season. This year, he had one less than the league-leader, Chuck Klein of the Cardinals. Ott also drove in 151 runs and hit for a .328 batting average. It was the beginning of a streak of eight consecutive years of driving in 100+ runs a season. The record stood for thirty years, until another pretty fair Giants hitter, Willie Mays, drove in 100+ runs from 1959-1966. Actually, Ott set yet another record for RBI's in 1929, when he managed to knock in twenty-seven runs in eleven consecutive games. His closest Major League competitor for this record was Babe Ruth, a distant second with eighteen RBIs in eleven consecutive games.

A little known fact about Ott is that he held a number of records for drawing bases-on-balls. He began one record in 1929 – the most years leading the league in walks (6). His streak of leading for three consecutive years (1931-1933) is also a record. Ruth holds the Major League record for career walks (2,036), Ott holds the National League mark with 1,708.

With catcher Shanty Hogan at .300, Edd Roush at .324, Lindstrom at .319 and a part-time catcher, Bob O'Farrell, at .306, the Giants had a potent attack. The pitching turned out to be the problem. Hubbell won eighteen games, including a no-hitter against Pittsburgh, but the rest of the staff did not deliver enough to bring McGraw another pennant.

Bill Walker and Freddie Fitzsimmons won fourteen and fifteen games respectively, but Benton slumped to an 11-17 record. Walker actually led the league in ERA with a 3.08, but it was the highest ERA ever to top the senior circuit.

The Dodgers suffered through another mediocre year, finishing sixth, with only seventy victories. Babe Herman, away from the pressure of playing first base, had a great year, hitting .381, knocking in 113 runs and belting twenty twenty-one homers. Johnny Frederick was also outstanding, batting .318 and leading the club in homers with twenty-four. Frederick also set two National League records for a rookie – most extra-base hits (82) and most total bases (342). In addition, Frederick set a Major League record for doubles by a rookie, fifty-two. Quite an auspicious debut for the youngster from Denver, Colorado, who had a brief, six-year career, all with Brooklyn, and finished with a .308 batting average.

Unfortunately, the Dodgers pitching was, once again, inadequate. Watty Clark won the most games (16), but also managed to lead the entire league in losses with nineteen. Most indicative of the pitching staff's poor performance was the fact that Clark "led" with a 3.74 ERA! Dazzy Vance slumped to a 14-13 mark, while Johnny Morrison and Ray Moss were the only other hurlers to win in double figures.

It was perhaps symbolic of the Dodgers mound problems that they brought in a rookie, twenty-one-year-old Bobo Newsom, and watched him painfully appear in three games, lose all three and post an ERA of 11.00! As it turned out, their faith in "Old Bobo," as he later became called, was justified. He would survive in the Major

Leagues for twenty-four more years and post 211 wins along the way. All of this while being traded sixteen times!

The Dodgers hit more doubles and triples than did the Giants, but had thirty-seven less homers, and drove in 124 less runs. The Dodgers pitchers led the league with 549 strikeouts, but the Giants hurlers gave up less hits and 162 less bases-on-balls. The Dodgers had now finished in sixth-place in seven of the past eight years. Even their most loyal fans had to feel that it was time to make some moves. In 1930, they did.

Dodgers		1929	Giants	
Babe Herman	.381	**BA**	Bill Terry	.372
" "	113	**RBI**	Mel Ott	151
Johnny Frederick	24	**HR**	" "	42
Watty Clark	16	**WINS**	Carl Hubbell	18
" "	3.74	**ERA**	Bill Walker	3.08*
" "	140	**SO**	Carl Hubbell	106

* led the National League

1930

Dazzy Vance Is 39-Year-Old Wonder

The Dodgers kept Del Bissonette from Winthorp, Maine at first base for the 1930 season. He had recovered from the injury that kept him out of forty-one games in 1929, and Del responded by hitting .336 in 146 games. But the Dodgers did change. Gone was aging shortstop Dave Bancroft, to the Giants, where McGraw played him for eight games at shortstop before releasing him. Glenn Wright had been picked up by Brooklyn the previous year in a trade with Pittsburgh and Wright produced; he played in 134 games, and hit .321 with twenty-two home runs (second on the club in homers to Babe Herman's 35). The Dodgers had a new catcher too – Al Lopez. Al had been up to the majors for a "cup of coffee" in 1928, but, after going 0-12, he wound up in the minors for the entire 1929 season. Now he had another chance and, at age twenty-one, he made the most of it. Lopez batted .309 in 128 games and showed maturity behind the plate that was beyond his years. (It came as no surprise to many that he became a manager for seventeen years when his active career as a player ended.)

Dazzy Vance surprised everyone by leading the club in wins (17), strikeouts (173), and complete games (20). He also managed to lead the league in shutouts with four and his ERA of 2.61 not only led the league, but was the only ERA in the National League below 3.00! Quite a year for a thirty-nine-year-old.

Besides his thirty-five homers, Babe Herman hit .393 to trail only Bill Terry, at .401, for the batting crown. It was the highest batting average *not* to win a batting title in Major League history. Frederick hit .334, and Bissonette added a .336 to contribute to the

Dodgers potent offense. All of this hitting carried them to a fourth-place finish, only six games behind pennant-winning St. Louis.

At 86-68, the Dodgers finished one game behind the Giants (87-67) and the battles between the two teams helped to take New Yorkers minds off of their troubles in this first full year of the Great Depression. Once again, the Giants hit more homers (143) than did Brooklyn (122), and knocked in more runs (880-836). The Giants team batting average was a Major League record, .319, which still stands today. The Dodgers weren't bad either at .304.

As mentioned, Bill Terry led the National League with a remarkable .401 batting average. No other National League batter has hit .400 since. Terry also led the league in hits with 254, runs scored, 139 and total bases, 392. All of these totals are still modern Major League records for a first baseman! Terry not only compiled an amazing number of batting records, but he also showed "Iron man" qualities by playing in all 154 games.

The Giants third baseman, Fred Lindstrom, had a great year too. He batted .379 and that, plus his 231 hits, are still Major League records for that position. He also led the club with 25 four-baggers. Travis Jackson and Shanty Hogan, both hit .339 and Freddie Leach was at .327 to round out a truly potent attack.

Despite the lively ball and the impressive offensive statistics being put up throughout the league, it was the Dodgers pitching that kept them in the hunt. While it does not sound impressive, their staff had a league-leading ERA of 4.03 in this year of the "suspect" baseball. (The Giants ERA was 4.60.) Four Brooklyn pitchers, in addition to Vance, won ten games or more. Phelps had a 14-7 record and Dolf Luque, "The Pride of Havana," was 14-8 at age thirty-nine. The Giants pitchers walked more batters, gave up more hits, struck out fewer and had only six shutouts to the Dodgers thirteen.

Obviously, the ball had been juiced up to attract a public that had been devastated by the onset of the depression. The effects were apparent in the statistics: the Phillies had a team-batting-average of .315, yet they fell from fourth to last place as their pitching staff's ERA ballooned to 6.71! The entire National League batted .303 (another record that still stands). It was a dream year for hitters and points up the achievement of the Dodgers staff to do as well as it did. As a final note, the Cubs Hack Wilson almost took advantage of the juiced up ball to eclipse Babe Ruth's home run record, but he was stopped at fifty-six.

Baseball was a good occupation in this first year of the Depression. The average player's salary was $7,000, somewhat skewed upward by Babe Ruth's phenomenal (for the times) compensation of $80,000. The Babe got all of that money only after a long holdout. The negotiations led to Ruth's famous response to a reporter's question: "Do you think that you deserve to be paid more than the President of the United States?" His retort was "Hell, yes. I had a better year than he did."

It would be the last year of the jack rabbit ball. Baseball would return to normalcy in 1931. Perhaps the results of this year's activities should have been assigned asterisks, as was Roger Maris' feat in surpassing the Babe's sixty home runs in 1961.

Dodgers	1930		Giants	
Babe Herman	.393	**BA**	Bill Terry	.401*
" "	130	**RBI**	" "	129
" "	35	**HR**	Mel Ott	25
Dazzy Vance	17	**WINS**	Freddie Fitzsimmons	19
" "	2.61*	**ERA**	Carl Hubbell	3.87
" "	173	**SO**	" "	117

* led the National League

1931

Dodgers Show their Age

After their rise to fourth-place, only six games out of first, in 1930, Dodgers fans were optimistic about their team's chances in 1931. Lefty O'Doul, who had batted .383 for the Phillies in the previous year, had come to Brooklyn. The Dodgers were also hoping for one more good year from their aging ace, Dazzy Vance; however, reality set in early.

The Cardinals were running away from the rest of the league and, eventually, led by the "Fordham Flash" Frankie Frisch, they would win the pennant by thirteen games over the second-place Giants. The Cubs finished third, four games ahead of Brooklyn. At age forty, the best that Vance could do was an 11-13 record. Considering that only two other Dodgers pitchers (Watty Clark (14) and Joe Shaute (11)) won more than ten games, that wasn't too bad.

With the demise of the jack rabbit ball of the previous year, batting records returned to normal. Newcomer O'Doul led the club with a .336 batting average and Babe Herman was at .313. Nobody on the club drove in 100 runs, although Herman came close with ninety-seven. He also led the team with seventeen stolen bases and set a record by hitting for the cycle three times in one season! No Dodgers reached twenty home runs and four of the regulars had a grand total of one home run between them!

Of Brooklyn's front-line pitchers, only one was under thirty, and two had reached forty. Jack Quinn, who was picked up from Philadelphia of the American League, appeared in fifteen games and won five of them at the advanced age of forty-eight! (In addition, he set a National League record for saves, at the time, with fifteen.)

110

A youth movement was definitely needed and the Dodgers did have one promising youngster. Van Lingle Mungo made his debut and, at age twenty, went 3-1 in five appearances. One of his wins was a shutout. The next year, he would join the regular rotation and make thirty-three starts.

The Giants had a good year, finishing second, four games ahead of the Cubs and eight games better than the Dodgers (87-65 to 79-73). Both were far behind the gaudy 101-53 posted by the Gashouse Gang of St. Louis. The Giants pitchers led the league in ERA with a 3.30 and four of them won ten games or more. However, no one won twenty, in a strange year for pitchers that did not produce a twenty-game winner in the entire league! Perhaps it was a delayed reaction to the barrage of hits in the previous year.

For the Giants, Fitzsimmons led the staff with eighteen wins. Bill Walker, from E. St. Louis, Missouri, followed with a 16-9 record and an ERA of 2.26 that led the league. He also led the league with six shutouts. Walker would throw nine more in a ten-year career with the Giants and Cardinals. Hubbell slumped to a 14-12 record, although his 2.65 ERA was second only to Walker's. McGraw was not averse to squeezing one more year out of a veteran. Forty-year-old lefthander, Clarence Mitchell was 13-11 for him and even started three games for the Giants in 1932 before retiring.

Bill Terry led the hitters once again for the Giants, but lost the league-batting title when Chick Hafey's .3489 topped his .3486. Hafey, of St. Louis, is also remembered for being the first batting crown winner ever to wear glasses.

As might be expected, Ott led the Giants in home runs with twenty-nine, but his batting average slipped to .292. Pitchers were showing a lot of respect for the twenty-two-year-old Ott and his odd batting style. He led the league in bases-on-balls with eighty. Jackson, Lindstrom, Leach and Hogan all hit .300 or better. Hogan was a great defensive catcher too. He set a new record for catchers in 1931 by posting an amazing .996 fielding average in 136 games behind the plate.

The Giants hit thirty more home runs and stole thirty-eight more bases than the Dodgers. Also, the Dodgers pitchers ERA was .54 higher than the Giants. There was little to hint at the change in fortunes to occur the following year.

Dodgers		1931	Giants	
Lefty O'Doul	.336	**BA**	Bill Terry	.348
Babe Herman	97	**RBI**	Mel Ott	115
" " "	18	**HR**	" "	29
Watty Clark	14	**WINS**	Freddie Fitzsimmons	18
" "	3.21	**ERA**	Bill Walker	2.26*
Dazzy Vance	150	**SO**	Carl Hubbell	156

* led the National League

1932

McGraw and Robinson Depart

1932 saw the surprising Dodgers rise to third place under new manager, Max Carey. Wilbert Robinson, who had managed the team since 1914 was gone. The team, which had been called the Robins for most of Wilbert's tenure, once again became the Dodgers – this time for good. In a surprising coincidence, forty games into the season, John McGraw stepped down as manager, turning the reins over to Bill Terry. McGraw had always admired Terry's subdued demeanor and fiery work ethic. It was a combination that would work well for Terry, the manager, as it did for Terry, the player. McGraw left a legacy of ten pennants and 4,878 wins in his thirty-three years at the helm. He brought the Giants home in the first division for twenty-eight of those thirty-three years.

An era had ended for both clubs. The Giants did not fare as well under Terry in 1932 as did the Dodgers with Max Carey. The Giants sank to a sixth-place tie with St. Louis, finishing thirty games out of first place – only Cincinnati was worse at 60-94.

For the Giants, two pitchers, Hubbell (18-11) and Fitzsimmons (11-11) won in double figures. Hi Bell, formerly of the Cardinals, but out of the Major Leagues the previous year, contributed an 8-4 record. The thirty-four-year-old right-hander from Mt. Sherman, Kentucky, proved to be a valuable spot starter and reliever for two more years. He had thirty-two wins and twenty-four saves by the time he retired at the end of the 1934 season.

As player-manager, Terry did his part on the field, playing in all 154 games at first base and batting a lusty .350, with twenty-eight home runs. Mel Ott also had a great year, hitting .318 and tying Chuck Klein of Philadelphia for National League leadership in homers with thirty-eight. Ott led the club with 123 RBI's and led the league with 100 bases-on-balls. Unfortunately, Jo Jo Moore was the team's only other .300 hitter at .305. In a minor highlight for the Giants, Sam Leslie out of Moss Point, Mississippi, set a record for the time of twenty-two pinch hits in a season.

The Dodgers rode O'Doul's league-leading .368 batting average and ninety RBI's to a third-place finish. Hack Wilson had come over from the Cubs and led the team in homers with 23 and in RBI's with 123. Both he and O'Doul had slugging averages above .500.

The pitching staff did their part too. Watty Clark won twenty games; Mungo had thirteen wins and both Sloppy Thurston and Dazzy Vance (at age forty-one) won twelve. Vance almost led the club in strikeouts, falling only four short as Van Lingle Mungo, twenty years his junior, beat him 107 to 103.

In addition to Hack Wilson, the Dodgers acquired Tony Cuccinello from the Reds. The Dodgers had sent Ernie Lombardi, Babe Herman and Wally Gilbert to the Reds for Cuccinello, Stripp and a future, long-time coach for the Dodgers, Clyde Sukeforth. Sukeforth was a light-hitting, but excellent defensive catcher, who quickly evidenced a knack for handling pitchers. He later garnered a perfect record as a Major League manager in 1947, when he won the one game that he led while the team waited for interim manager, Burt Shotton, to arrive.

Cuccinello, out of Queens in New York City, played all 154 games for the Dodgers at second base and hit a respectable .281. Joe Stripp hit .303 and Al Lopez, finally settling in as the Dodgers catcher, at age twenty-three, handled the pitching staff beautifully, while batting .275. He was destined to play, and then manage, for thirty-seven more years.

The Giants out-hit the Dodgers in almost every category, but the boys from Brooklyn had a combination of veterans and youngsters who knew how to win. Johnny Frederick, for example, had sixteen homers, but six were pinch-hits at crucial moments in a game. (At the time, the six pinch-hit homers set a Major League record.)

Who would have expected the teams to once again reverse fortunes the following year?

Dodgers	1932	Giants	
Lefty O'Doul	.368*	**BA**	Bill Terry	.350
Hack Wilson	123	**RBI**	Mel Ott	123
" " "	23	**HR**	" "	38*
Watty Clark	20	**WINS**	Carl Hubbell	18
" "	3.49	**ERA**	" " "	2.50
Van Lingle Mungo	107	**SO**	" " "	137

* led the National League

1933

Terry Leads Giants to Pennant

The combination of Bill Terry's leadership and performance on the field paid off in 1933 as the Giants leaped from sixth-place, eighteen games back the previous year, to a pennant. Terry hit .322 and, with Mel Ott providing the power (23 homers and 103 RBI's), and Carl Hubbell as the mainstay of its pitching staff, the Giants finished five games ahead of Pittsburgh and six games ahead of the previous year's champion Chicago Cubs. Hubbell's contribution included a Major League-leading twenty-three wins; a league-leading 1.66 ERA; 309 innings pitched and recognition at the end of the season as the National League's Most Valuable Player.

In addition to his ERA being the best in the Major Leagues since the introduction of the lively ball, Hubbell's ten shutouts were the most in the majors since the great Peter Alexander in 1916 had sixteen! In the current age of middle-and-late-relief pitching, we can justly tip our caps to Hubbell's performance of August 2nd of this year when one of his ten shutouts was a complete game, an eighteen-inning affair, against St. Louis. (Perhaps, he should have been awarded credit for two shutouts for that outing!)

Some thought that Terry had done it with mirrors. The Giants team batting average of .263 was no better than that of the sixth-place Dodgers. Terry was the team's only .300 hitter and the club was barely fourth in RBI's. As might be expected, however, given the dimensions of the Polo Grounds, they did lead the league in home runs with eighty-two.

The key to their success was the pitching staff. In addition to Hubbell's exploits, the staff led the Major Leagues in shutouts with twenty-three, had the lowest ERA, 2.71, and were second in strikeouts to Dizzy Dean's Cardinals with 555. They gave up the least hits in the Majors (1,280); by comparison, the pennant-winning Washington Senators in the American League gave up 1,415!)

A major reason for the Giants pitching resurgence was the emergence of (Prince Hal) Schumacher. In his third year with the Giants, at age twenty-two, the youngster from Hinchley, New York found his stuff and made the rest of the league pay. Schumacher went 19-12. Freddie Fitzsimmons was still effective at 16-11 and Roy Parmalee, who had been 3-6 in four prior years with the club, finally rewarded their patience with thirteen wins, only eight losses, and 132 strikeouts. Hubbell led the club with 156.

There was more to this pitching staff. Dolf-Adolfo Luque, known as "The Pride of Havana," had joined the Giants the previous year as a well-traveled forty-one-year old. At age forty-two, in 1933, he showed some of his youthful spark by going 8-2 with a 2.70 ERA. It may have been Hubbell's year, but the rest of the staff clearly helped.

Hubbell and Schumacher made short work of Washington in the World Series. Each won two games in a five-game Giants romp. (Washington scored a total of only eleven runs in the Series.) Hubbell had the remarkable ERA of 0.00 in his two wins. It was a bitter loss for the Senators, who had beaten out the Yankees by seven full games to take the American League flag. Who would have guessed at the time that it would be the last appearance ever for Washington in a World Series?

The Dodgers, meanwhile, were back in their accustomed sixth-place, for the twelfth time in twenty-eight years. Johnny Frederick and Al Lopez managed to hit .300, but no one on the club hit more than nine home runs and the team's RBI total was seventy less than in the prior year. The team batting average sank twenty points to .263 and their pitching staff's ERA was a full 1.02 higher than the Giants at 3.73. Van Lingle Mungo led a mediocre staff performance with a record of 16-15 and an ERA of 2.72. The other starters all had records under .500. Ownie Carroll was 13-15, Boom Boom Beck was 12-20 and Ray Benge was 10-17. All in all, it was a year that manager Max Carey, and the Dodgers fans, would just as soon forget.

Dodgers		1933	Giants	
Johnny Frederick	.308	**BA**	Bill Terry	.322
Tony Cuccinello	65	**RBI**	Mel Ott	103
" " "	9	**HR**	" "	23
Danny Taylor				
Van Lingle Mungo	16	**WINS**	Carl Hubbell	23*
" " " " "	2.72	**ERA**	" " "	1.66*
" " " " "	110	**SO**	" " "	156

* led the National League

1934

Casey Stengel "Leads" the Dodgers

The Dodgers added to their record of sixth-place finishes by landing there again in 1934. As Ebbets Field dwellers, they would finish sixth only once more before departing for California in 1958. Sam Leslie, a first baseman traded to the Dodgers by the Giants in 1933, had a banner year. He led the club with a .332 batting average in 146 games.

There were other new faces contributing to the same old result. Lonny Frey, who had played thirty-four games at shortstop for Brooklyn in 1933, took over the position at age twenty-two, from an aging Glenn Wright. Wright ended his career the following year with the Chicago White Sox, appearing in only nine games. Buzz Boyle had played in only twenty-five games the previous year. Given a chance to play regularly, the outfielder responded by batting .305. Len Koenecke, another outfielder who had a "cup of coffee" with the Giants in 1932, and spent 1933 in the minors, was purchased by the Dodgers. It turned out to be a good investment as Koenecke hit .320 with fourteen homers. (Tragically, Koenecke, from Baraboo, Wisconsin, died in September of 1935 at age thirty-one.)

On the mound for Brooklyn, Van Lingle Mungo, out of Pageland, South Carolina, once again led an undistinguished pitching staff. He led the league in games started, but also led in hits allowed (300) and walks (104). Mungo finished the season at 18-16. Ray Benge and Dutch Leonard each won fourteen, but the rest of the staff was ineffective. Only Philadelphia had a worse ERA (4.76) than the Dodgers (4.48).

The Dodgers had a new manager in 1934 – Casey Stengel. It was the first managerial job for the man who would later become known as the "Ol' Professor." Casey had produced a respectable record as a player with the Giants, Braves and Phillies. He would, of course, be heard from later as manager of the Yankees and the expansion New York Mets.

The Giants slipped to second place as the "Gashouse Gang" – Durocher, Frisch, Pepper Martin, Joe Medwick and the Dean brothers – gave St. Louis the pennant by two games. It was a great disappointment for a Giants team that had led the National League for 127 consecutive days before being overtaken by the Cardinals. The Cards then went on to surprise the favored Detroit Tigers, with Gehringer, Greenberg and Cochran, by winning the World Series, four games to three.

Hal Schumacher led the Giants pitching staff with a 23-10 mark; right behind him was Hubbell at 21-12. Fitzsimmons chipped in eighteen wins and Roy Parmalee had ten before being injured. Hubbell's 2.30 ERA once again led the National League. He also managed to lead the league in saves with eight. This was the year that Hubbell starred in the All-Star Game by striking out five consecutive batters. They happened to be: Ruth, Gehrig, Foxx, Simmons and Cronin – all future Hall-of-Famers!

Bill Terry had another sensational year. He hit .354, with 213 hits in 153 games. Ott batted .326 and once again led the National League in home runs with thirty-five – actually, a tie with the Cardinals Ripper Collins. Ott did top all National Leaguers with 135 RBI's. Jo Jo Moore contributed a .331 batting average and 192 hits, but it wasn't enough for the Giants to grab a second consecutive pennant. Even Lefty O'Doul, serving as a part-time player at age thirty-seven, and hitting .316, couldn't put them over the top.

The sixth-place Dodgers played a role in preventing the Giants from outlasting the Cardinals. On September 29th, as Paul Dean of

St. Louis was beating Cincinnati, the Dodgers beat the Giants and the Cardinals got a lead that they never relinquished. The Dodgers won the next day too. Some pundits say that the Dodgers victories over the Giants at the end of the season were in retribution for Bill Terry's pre-season comment when asked about the Dodgers chances for the coming year: "Is Brooklyn still in the league?"

Dodgers		1934	Giants	
Sam Leslie	.332	**BA**	Bill Terry	.354
" " "	102	**RBI**	Mel Ott	135*
Tony Cuccinello Len Koenecke	14	**HR**	" "	35*
Van Lingle Mungo	18	**WINS**	Hal Schumacher	23
Dutch Leonard	3.28	**ERA**	Carl Hubbell	2.30*
Van Lingle Mungo	184	**SO**	" " "	118

* led the National League

1935

Hubbell Continues his Mastery

In 1935, the Dodgers moved up a notch to fifth-place, while the Giants were slipping to third. Still, the Giants were a first-division club and Carl Hubbell, at age thirty-two, was still the master. He won twenty-three games to lead the Giants staff, while losing twelve. He was always known for his control and this year he walked only forty-nine batters, while striking out 150. He had only one shutout (he had five the year before), but his 3.27 ERA was respectable and he knew how to win.

This was the year that Babe Ruth was ungraciously released by the Yankees, because of his age (40), and picked up by the Boston Braves – mainly to improve their anemic attendance. The Braves also knew that with their current collection of players they needed a miracle, and even an aged Babe might be it. For a brief moment, it looked like the miracle might occur. In his first at-bat as a Brave, against none other than Carl Hubbell, the Babe homered! Unfortunately, reality soon set in and by June it was over. Ruth had only hit five more homers and was batting .181. The Braves ended up in the National League basement, with 115 losses, although ironically, they did have the league's home run leader – Wally Berger belted 34 homers for a team that won only thirty-eight games.

The Giants pitching staff also featured Hal Schumacher. He was brilliant again, with a 19-9 won-lost record and a 2.89 ERA. Slick Castleman, out of Donelson, Tennessee, made his debut and contributed a sparkling 15-6 record. Not bad for a twenty-one-year-old. Unfortunately, Slick won only eleven more games in the next five years and was out of baseball after 1939. Parmalee was 14-10, but both he and Castleman had ERA's above 4.00. Parmalee also managed to lead the league in bases-on-balls with ninety-seven. (That was forty-eight more walks than Hubbell gave up, despite pitching seventy-seven more innings!)

There was nothing wrong with the Giants hitting. They posted a team batting average of .286, only two percentage points lower than the pennant-winning Cubs and two points better than the second-place Cardinals. Bill Terry, at age thirty-six, was still the leader both on and off the field; he hit .341. The much traveled Mark Koenig, who had starred with the fabled 1927 Yankees and then been supplanted at shortstop by such "stars" as Leo Durocher in 1929, and Lyn Lary in 1930, played 107 games for the Giants and hit a respectable .283. Mel Ott hit .322, with thirty-one homers and 141 RBI's. In addition, Hank Leiber got a chance to play regularly, and the twenty-four-year-old outfielder, from Phoenix, Arizona, hit .331, with twenty-two home runs and 107 RBI's. (He was the second-best RBI man on the club, with Ott, of course, the first.)

Joe Malay, from Brooklyn, New York, was an interesting story. He had briefly played first base for the Giants in 1933 and then was sent down to the minors. He came up again in 1935, batted once (a single) and never played another day in the Major Leagues. I am sure that in future years, he treasured that base hit. The story for the Giants in 1935 was that they were good, but the Cardinals and Cubs were just a little better.

The Dodgers escaped their sixth-place rut, by moving up to fifth-place. This, despite the fact that only two of their pitchers, Mungo and Clark, won in double figures. In fact, the pitching staff had a horrible ERA of 4.22. Manager Casey Stengel tried no less than sixteen pitchers during the course of the season, including grizzled veterans like forty-four-year-old Dazzy Vance, who went 3-2, with an ERA of 4.41. Also in the mix was thirty-nine-year-old Tom Zachary. Tom compiled a record of 7-12, with a 3.59 ERA. An attempt by Casey to inject some youth into the rotation didn't help much either. Twenty-two year-old Johnny Babick was 7-14, with a horrendous ERA of 6.67 in 143 innings, and a nineteen-year-old Harry Eisenstat, (later to achieve fame and respect as a "man in blue!") appeared in two games, lost one and posted an ERA of 12.60! Actually, Eisenstat hung around as a "spot" pitcher for twelve years. He won twenty-five games, lost twenty-seven, and brought his ERA down to 3.83 before he was done.

It would take a lot of good hitting to compensate for that pitching staff, and the Dodgers just did not have enough of it to crack the first division. They ended up sixteen games behind fourth place Pittsburgh. Sam Leslie, Joe Stripp and Jim Bucher all hit .300, but that was it for the offense. In fact, Leslie was the only one of the three who played regularly. Lonny Frey, at 5'10" and 160 pounds, led the club with eleven homers. In a fifteen-year career, Lonny hit only fifty more.

Dodgers		1935	Giants	
Sam Leslie	.308	**BA**	Bill Terry	.341
" " "	93	**RBI**	Mel Ott	114
Lonny Frey	11	**HR**	" "	31
Van Lingle Mungo	16	**WINS**	Carl Hubbell	23
Watty Clark	3.30	**ERA**	Hal Schumacher	2.89
Van Lingle Mungo	143	**SO**	Carl Hubbell	150

1936

Ott and Hubbell Star

In retrospect, 1935 was probably a good experience for Casey Stengel in preparation for 1962 and the brand new New York Mets. The Dodgers, like the future Mets, never gave Casey much in the way of talent to work with. It certainly would have been hard for Casey to imagine in 1935 what glory lay ahead for him in 1949 when he donned the pinstripes of the New York Yankees as manager. It would have been even harder in 1936.

1936 saw the Dodgers slide all the way to seventh-place – a full twenty-five games behind the pennant-winning Giants. Bill Terry, in earning his second flag in four full years as manager, had been hobbled by a knee injury and appeared in only seventy-nine games. He still hit .310 and drove in thirty-nine runs.

Former Giants first baseman, Sam Leslie, who had been exiled to the Dodgers for two seasons, returned and filled in respectably for Terry. He hit .295 in 117 games. Mel Ott was, once again, the hitting star. He led the league with thirty-three home runs and a .588 slugging average. He also drove in 135 runs; second in the league to Ducky Medwick of St. Louis, who had 138. Jo Jo Moore and catcher, Gus Mancuso, also topped .300, but it was Carl Hubbell who stepped up with another sensational year that pushed the Giants to the pennant. King Carl went 26-6 to lead the league in wins and winning percentage. In addition, his ERA of 2.31 was tops in the majors. It clearly helped the Giants pennant run to have a pitching staff that led the Major Leagues in ERA with a 3.46.

Hubbell had a remarkable streak, that actually began in 1935, of winning twenty-four consecutive games. To illustrate his importance to the club – the Giants were 92-62 on the year, but only 66-56 when Hubbell was not on the mound! Four other Giants hurlers were winners of ten games or more, although Schumacher had a surprisingly poor season, finishing with an 11-13 mark.

The pennant race was an exciting one. In a dramatic, three-team race, the Giants jumped out in front of the Cubs by putting together a fifteen-game winning streak in late July. Then, in a clutch series at the end of August, the Giants took three of four from the Cubs, who had roared past the Giants, into first place in June, by reeling off fifteen consecutive wins themselves.

In a repeat of the 1923 World Series, the Giants and Yankees squared off and once again, the Yankees were the victors, four games to two. Schumacher was better in the post-season. He accounted for both of the Giants wins, including a 10-inning victory in Game Five.

Meanwhile, the Dodgers spent the year floundering in the second division. Stengel had a few bright spots, such as rookie Buddie Hassett, another product of the New York City sandlots, playing 156 games at first base and batting .310. Hassett set a Major League record for rookies by striking out just seventeen times in 635 at-bats. (By 1942, Hassett was a Yankee, hitting .333 in the World Series. World War II then intervened and Hassett never made it back to the Major Leagues.)

Joe Stripp, from Harrison, New Jersey, had another good year for Brooklyn, batting .317 and Frenchy Bordagray contributed a .315. The brightest spot, in this dismal season, came from an unexpected source. Catcher Babe Phelps, a career .300 hitter, outdid himself by batting .367 in 115 games – a modern Major League record for a catcher. Unfortunately for Phelps, future Hall-of-Famer Paul Waner hit .373 to lead the league.

A couple of well-traveled hurlers had joined the Dodgers for the season. Fred Frankhouse, at age thirty-two, was 13-10 and Ed

Brandt went 11-13. They joined Van Lingle Mungo (18-19) as the only Brooklyn pitchers to win more than seven games. Mungo led all of the Major Leagues with 238 strikeouts. Unfortunately, he also led his own league in walks with 118. He was a major contributor to the Dodgers leading the National League in walks with 528 as well as in strikeouts, 651.

More hitting would certainly have helped the beleaguered Dodgers staff. The team total of thirty-three homers barely equaled Mel Ott's individual performance. (Babe Phelps led them with five!)

Dodgers		1936	Giants	
Babe Phelps	.367	**BA**	Mel Ott	.328
Buddy Hassett	82	**RBI**	" "	135
Babe Phelps	5	**HR**	" "	33*
Van Lingle Mungo	18	**WINS**	Carl Hubbell	26*
" " " " "	3.35	**ERA**	" " " "	2.31*
" " " " "	238*	**SO**	" " " "	123

* led the National League

127

The Giants celebrate capturing their second consecutive pennant in 1937.

1937

Terry Does It Again

Bill Terry led the Giants to the National League flag again in 1937. It was his third pennant in five full seasons as manager. This was his first as a full-time bench manager, but Johnny McCarthy filled in decently at first base – as much as anyone could in trying to replace an all-star like Terry – and, as usual, Mel Ott carried the team with his bat.

Ott led the National League once again in home runs, with thirty-one, and bases-on-balls with 102. (Actually, he tied for the home run lead with Ducky Medwick of the Cardinals, who had a sensational year at the plate, culminating in a Triple Crown.) Three Giants had good years – Dick Bartell (.306), Jimmy Ripple (.317) and Jo Jo Moore (.310), but it was the pitching, yet again, which brought them the flag.

Hubbell led the league in wins with twenty-two; strikeouts (159); and winning percentage (.733). He lost only eight games, and had four shutouts. The rubber-armed screwballer was second in the National League in innings pitched (262) and led his own club in games started (32).

Cliff Melton, a twenty-five-year-old rookie from Brevard, North Carolina, with the nickname "Mountain Music," made a sensational debut in the big leagues by posting a 20-9 record and a 2.61 ERA. He also contributed seven saves to tie him for the league lead. Schumacher, Castleman (before he went on the injured list) and Harry Gumbert all won in double figures too.

The World Series was once again a rout, as the powerhouse Yankees took the Giants in five games, while outscoring them 28-12. Jo Jo Moore was a bright spot for the Giants, collecting nine hits and a .391 batting average. Future Hall-of-Famer, Tony Lazzeri starred for the Yankees with six hits in fifteen at-bats, for a .400 Series performance. George Selkirk had six RBI's and scored five runs to help rout the Giants. Lou Gehrig added a homer and three RBI's. It would be the last World Series homer for the great first baseman of the New York Yankees.

In 1937, Casey Stengel was gone from the Dodgers and from Major League baseball. Burleigh Grimes, known as "Ol' Stubblebeard," had taken over the club and, in doing so, returned to the scene of some of his greatest pitching moments. Unfortunately, there was no Burleigh Grimes on the current Dodgers roster. Luke Hamlin at 11-13, Max Butcher, 11-15, and Fred Frankhouse at 10-13, led a lackluster staff. The team's ERA was an inflated 4.13. (The Giants, by comparison, finished at 3.43.) They also scored 116 more runs than Brooklyn did and hit seventy-four more home runs. (111-37)

The Dodgers did start to rebuild in 1937, while finally completing their last year in sixth-place as residents of Ebbets Field. Cookie Lavagetto was brought up from the minors and the utility infielder hit .282. A young outfielder, from Toronto, Canada, named Goody Rosen, got seventy-seven at-bats and hit .312. That won him a starting job the following year. Buddy Hassett had another good year at .304. Heinie Manush, nearing the end of a career that saw him achieve a lifetime batting average of .330, was acquired from the Red Sox and, true to form, hit .333 in 132 games. Babe Phelps took over from Ray Beres as regular catcher and hit .313, but none of this offense was enough to overcome the weak pitching and lack of power. In the off-season, in another move, the Dodgers picked up a weak-hitting, but fiery field leader of a shortstop from St. Louis called Leo Durocher. The lad from W. Springfield, Massachusetts would be heard from later, and so would the perennial second-division Dodgers. Their time was coming.

Dodgers		1937	Giants	
Heinie Manush	.333	**BA**	Jimmy Ripple	.317
" " " "	73	**RBI**	Mel Ott	95
Cookie Lavagetto	8	**HR**	" "	31*
Luke Hamlin Max Butcher	11	**WINS**	Carl Hubbell	22*
Van Lingle Mungo	2.91	**ERA**	Cliff Melton	2.61
" " " " "	122	**SO**	Carl Hubbell	159*

* led the National League

The lights went on at Ebbets Field in 1938, but Vander Meer stole the spotlight.

1938

No-hitter "Electrifies" Dodgers Fans

Dolf Camilli, the slugging first baseman of the Phillies, had been acquired by the Dodgers during the off-season and, in his first year, proved to be as productive as had been hoped. The thirty-one-year old, left-handed batter, hit twenty-four homers – an impressive number on a team that had a total of thirty-seven in 1937. Big Dolf quickly became a fan favorite as he found the nearby, right field scoreboard to be friendly. He rapped twenty-five doubles, many of them off that scoreboard, and led the club with one hundred RBI's. This made Camilli the first Brooklyn player to drive in one hundred runs since Sam Leslie turned the trick in 1934.

Unfortunately, Camilli got little help from his teammates. Rookie Ernie Koy, out of Sealy, Texas, had eleven home runs and hit .299, but that was as close as any Dodgers hitter got to .300.

On the mound, southpaw Vito Tamulis, from Cambridge, Massachusetts, had won ten games for the Yankees in 1935 and then disappeared from the Major Leagues. The desperate Dodgers bought his contract from the Cardinals and Tamulis shocked everybody by tying Luke Hamlin for most wins on the club with a twelve and six record. Freddie Fitzsimmons, in his second year as a Dodger and beginning to earn his nickname of "Fat Freddy," was still effective at age thirty-six. He posted an 11-8 record. Tot Pressnell, a thirty-one-year-old rookie from Findlay, Ohio, won eleven games, while losing fourteen. The pitching was generally mediocre. The staff posted an ERA of 4.07, had next-to-the-last number of strikeouts in the league with 469 and turned in the fewest complete games in the league, fifty-six.

Brooklyn understandably finished a dismal seventh. They were lucky in that the Phillies were so bad that they finished a distant twenty-five and a half games behind the Dodgers. (The Phillies won only forty-five games all year.) As usual, the manager was blamed for the team's poor performance and Burleigh Grimes was fired at the end of the season. He never managed in the Major Leagues again. (The Phillies manager was fired too.)

The Giants had another good year, but not good enough to overtake the Cubs. Chicago won the pennant by two games over Pittsburgh and five over New York. To no one's surprise, Ott led the league with thirty-six home runs. He also drove in 116 runs and hit .311. As if his hitting was not enough, Ott voluntarily played 113 games at third base to help the team. He also posted a seventh consecutive year of playing at least 150 games out of a 154 game schedule.

It puzzles this writer that Ott was never selected to receive a National League Most Valuable Player Award. Apparently he was so consistently great, for so long, that the writers just took him for granted when they cast their votes.

The Most Valuable Player Award began to be given in 1931 and Carl Hubbell, who had won it in 1933 and 1936, was clearly approaching the end of his brilliant career by 1938. (Pitchers competed with everyday players for the honor until the Cy Young Award, specifically for pitchers, began to be awarded in 1956.) He appeared in twenty-four games, twenty-two as a starter, and achieved a respectable 13-10 record. He also managed to lead the Giants staff in strikeouts with 104. Despite throwing a screwball, Hubbell never suffered from a sore arm as an active player, but his arm later became permanently distorted from throwing that difficult pitch. It amazed most observers of the game that his arm lasted as long as it did.

Harry Gumbert, the pride of Elizabeth, Pennsylvania, led the Giants staff in wins with fifteen. Melton won fourteen and

Schumacher won thirteen. Dick Coffman, from Veto, Alabama, may have rescued the Giants from a second division finish by saving twelve games in relief. He was the National League leader in that category. Coffman also had a fine 8-4 won-lost record. Jo Jo Moore, and second-year catcher, Harry Danning, hit over .300 and the Giants led the league in home runs with 125. All in all, it was a better than average year for the Giants, but not one of pennant winning quality.

A highlight of 1938 was Johnny Vander Meer's posting of two consecutive no-hitters for Cincinnati; a feat that has never been duplicated. The Dodgers had the misfortune of being the left-hander's second victim. It happened on June 15th, which also coincided with the first night game ever played at Ebbets Field. To add to that dramatic touch, it was also the first year that the Dodgers and Giants allowed their home games to be broadcast on the radio. Besides the full house at the park for the initial night game, many thousands of fans sat glued to their radios to hear if Vander Meer could do it again. Could anyone have written a better script for the Dodgers first game under the lights?

Two events would occur during the off-season which would affect both the Dodgers and the Giants. The Giants traded the "glue" of their infield, Dick Bartell, catcher Gus Mancuso and outfielder Hank Leiber to the Cubs for Billy Jurges, Frank Demaree and Ken O'Dea. The Dodgers hired Larry McPhail as general manager. The repercussions from both of these events would become visible at once in 1939.

Dodgers		1938	Giants	
Ernie Koy	.299	**BA**	Mel Ott	.311
Dolph Camilli	100	**RBI**	" "	116
" " " "	24	**HR**	" "	36*
Luke Hamlin Vito Tamulis	12	**WINS**	Harry Gumbert	15
Freddie Fitzsimmons	3.01	**ERA**	Carl Hubbell	3.07
Luke Hamlin	97	**SO**	" " "	104

* led the National League

1939

Durocher Goes to Work

1939 saw the return of the Dodgers to the first division for the first time since 1932. With the exception of the 1944 season, with its depleted wartime rosters, they would be a first-division team for the remainder of their stay in Brooklyn.

In one of general manager Larry McPhail's early moves, Leo Durocher was named player-manager. Leo, who had hit only .219 in his initial year with the Dodgers, responded by, not only driving the team to a third-place finish, but by hitting .277 (thirty points above his lifetime average). The entire team responded to Leo's enthusiasm and pugnaciousness. After six consecutive seasons in the second division, it was intoxicating to be winning for a change.

They topped eighty wins for the first time since 1932, going 84-69, and finishing six games ahead of the Giants, who had fallen to fifth-place; coincidentally, their first time in the second division since that same 1932. The fortunes of the two teams had taken a dramatic turn that would see the Dodgers prosper in the first division, while the Giants would wallow in the second division for seven of the next eight years.

Besides Durocher's leadership, there were many reasons for the Dodgers success. Luke Hamlin, at thirty-four, had twenty wins and Hugh Casey, whom McPhail plucked from the Cubs, won fifteen. In another shrewd move, McPhail brought over a ten-year veteran from the American League named John Whitlow Wyatt – forever more known as "Whit." At age thirty-one, he had an undistinguished record, even being released by Cleveland at the end of the 1937 season; he had been 2-3 for them, with a 4.44 ERA. No one picked him up for 1938; most general managers assumed that the Kensington, Georgia native was washed up – not McPhail.

Whitlow quickly took advantage of his good fortune and became a favorite with Dodgers fans. He was 8-3 in 1939 and had a sparkling 2.31 ERA, with a team-tying two shutouts. Other good things happened to the team. Camilli continued his slugging: he hit twenty-six homers and was feared enough by opposing teams to draw a league-leading 110 walks. The free-swinging Camilli also led the league in strikeouts with 107. Both of his totals helped the Dodgers to lead the league in those categories.

Cookie Lavagetto, another Oakland, California product, became a fixture at third base and hit .300 with ten home runs. Pete Coscorart and Leo Durocher became a smooth double-play combo and the mixture of good pitching, solid defense and timely hitting all contributed to the successful season. The Dodgers were no longer the league clowns, but a team respected for playing smart, aggressive baseball. Durocher deserves most of the credit for that.

Meanwhile, the Giants, despite having five of their pitchers win in double figures (Harry Gumbert led with an 18-11 season) saw their pitching staff's ERA rise from 3.64 in 1938 to 4.07 in 1939. At age thirty-six, "King Carl" still was effective. He contributed 154 innings and led the staff with an ERA of 2.75. Coincidentally, the Dodgers did exactly the reverse – going from a 4.07 ERA in 1938 to 3.64 in 1939! Mel Ott was still "Mr. Reliable," batting .308, hitting twenty-seven homers and drawing one hundred bases-on-balls. It was not nearly enough to prevent a fifth place finish – 18 ½ games behind Cincinnati.

Zeke Bonura out of New Orleans, Louisiana, had been picked up by the Giants from the Washington Senators and hit .321, with eleven home runs. On July 8th and 9th, he had the misfortune of setting a Major League record by hitting into five consecutive double plays! Despite having been the Giants leading hitter for average, big Zeke was traded back to Washington at the end of the season. The Giants planned to try out their newest "phenom," Babe Young, at first base for 1940. In addition, the Giants had picked up Frank Demaree from the Cubs and he responded with a .304 batting average and seventy-nine RBI's. Harry Danning caught 135 games and batted .313 with sixteen homers.

The Giants led the league in homers with 116 and actually had a team-batting average higher (by one point) than the previous year, when they finished third. Statistically, the Giants had a pretty good year, but something was wrong. For the second consecutive year, they had dropped two places in the league standings. 1939 also marked the first year that the Dodgers batters had knocked in more runs than did the Giants since 1925 (653-651).

Dodgers		1939	Giants	
Cookie Lavagetto	.300	**BA**	Zeke Bonura	.321
Dolph Camilli	104	**RBI**	" "	85
" " " "	26	**HR**	Mel Ott	27
Luke Hamlin	20	**WINS**	Harry Gumbert	18
Hugh Casey	2.93	**ERA**	Carl Hubbell	2.75
Luke Hamlin	88	**SO**	Cliff Melton	95

1940

Pee Wee Takes Over

The Dodgers had their best start ever in 1940. They won their first eight games and in their ninth, Tex Carleton – who would turn thirty-four later in the season, and who, after six years with the Cardinals and Cubs had dropped into the minor leagues the previous season – pitched a no-hitter against the powerhouse Cincinnati Reds. However, things soon returned to normal. The Reds, with tremendous hitting and superb pitching ran away from Brooklyn to win the pennant by twelve games.

A sad footnote to the Reds victory was the tale of second-string catcher Willard Hershberger. Called upon to fill in for the injured regular, Ernie Lombardi, he succumbed to the pennant pressure in August and committed suicide. Hershberger had a .316 batting average in his three seasons with the Reds and had played in 160 games. He was thirty years old. Interestingly, when Lombardi re-injured himself, forty-year-old coach, Jimmy Wilson, was activated. He finished the season behind the plate and starred in the World Series both defensively and at bat. He hit .353 as the Reds won over Detroit in seven games to become world champions. People noticed and the following year Wilson was named manager of the Chicago Cubs. Two dramatically different results stemmed from injuries to the same ballplayer.

For the Dodgers, Carleton finished 6-6 as reality set in for him too. Tex never pitched another season in the Major Leagues. Still, Brooklyn had moved up to second place. Freddie Fitzsimmons, at age thirty-eight, was an incredible 16-2 with a league-leading percentage of .889. The rest of the staff, led by Whit Wyatt's 124, was tops in the league in strikeouts, 639, and shutouts, seventeen.

Wyatt, the thirty-year old castoff had become an ace, and proven general manager Larry McPhail to be a genius. Wyatt won fifteen games. Hugh Casey won eleven and five other pitchers contributed at least six wins apiece.

Dolf Camilli once again paced the club in homers with twenty-three and newly acquired Ducky Medwick, who came over from the Cardinals, along with pitcher Curt Davis, hit seventeen. Dixie Walker, "The People's Cherce," recovered from a knee injury that had hampered him in 1939. He played in 136 games and hit .308. Two youngsters also arrived, who were to have an impact and capture the imagination of the fans.

An era ended as one of them, the "Kentucky Colonel," later simply, "the Captain," Pee Wee Reese replaced Leo Durocher at shortstop on April 24th. He played at that position for eighty-four games before breaking a bone in his foot. The other newcomer, Pete Reiser, playing some third base, shortstop and the outfield, appeared in fifty-eight games and hit .293. Their glory days were ahead of them.

Durocher, at age thirty-four, was still a playing manager, filling in for the injured Reese at shortstop for fifty-three games, plus four games at second base. It was a far cry from the 116 games that he had played in the year before. To all intents and purposes, Leo's playing days, and the aura of the old "Gashouse Gang," were over – at least, on the field..

The Giants dropped another notch in 1940 to sixth-place, despite a team batting average that was higher than both the Reds and the Dodgers. Schumacher led the Giants staff in wins (13-13), while five others won ten or more: Hubbell, at age thirty-seven, was 11-12; Gumbert was 12-14; Lohrman went 10-15 and Melton was 10-11 (with an ERA of 4.90!) The staff's ERA was a hefty 3.79. Giants pitchers gave up 1,383 hits, which was third best in the National League, but despite this and a good team batting average, things never came together for this club. They finished 27½ games behind Cincinnati with a 72-80 record. Frank Demaree and Harry Danning were their only .300 hitters as Ott slipped to a total of only nineteen homers and seventy-nine RBI's. Babe Young led the club in RBI's with 101 and hit seventeen homers.

Dodgers		1940	Giants	
Dixie Walker	.308	**BA**	Frank Demaree	.302
Dolph Camilli	96	**RBI**	Babe Young	101
" " " "	23	**HR**	Mel Ott	19
Freddie Fitzsimmons	16	**WINS**	Hal Schumacher	13
" " " "	2.82	**ERA**	" " " "	3.25
Whit Wyatt	124	**SO**	" " " "	123

1941

Brooklyn Mourns "Passed Ball"

While the Giants would continue their tenure in the second division in 1941, the Dodgers, who had added another piece to their puzzle with the acquisition of catcher Mickey Owen from the Cardinals, for Gus Mancuso and cash, were ready. Larry McPhail had made the right moves and 1941 was clearly the Dodgers year of opportunity.

Larry McPhail's genius at finding the right player for the right position amazed the baseball world. In only three years he had converted a perpetual, second division club into a contender. His final move was to add more power at second base – a baseball tradition since Rogers Hornsby. He did so by getting Billy Herman from Chicago for outfielder Augie Galan. Herman's solid fielding and hitting (he batted .291, with thirty doubles) plus his veteran presence alongside the youngster, Reese, at shortstop, helped lift the Dodgers all the way to the top of the National League for the first time in twenty-one years. Augie Galan, also acquired from the Cubs, proved to be a valuable outfielder throughout the war years.

Brooklyn had many other heroes. Camilli had a great year, with league leading stats in homers (34), RBI's (120) and, on the negative side, strikeouts (115). Pete Reiser, out of St. Louis, burst upon the baseball scene like a meteor. In his first full year, "Pistol Pete" led the National League in: batting average (.343); slugging average (.558); triples (17) and doubles (39). At twenty-two, he was the youngest ever to lead the league in batting. The combination of his speed, power and recklessness – especially a propensity for crashing into the, as yet, unpadded outfield walls – electrified the Dodgers faithful and energized the ball club.

Dixie Walker and Joe Medwick both hit over .300, but it was in team achievements that the Dodgers really dominated. They led the league in: home runs (101); triples (69); doubles (286); hits (1,494); runs scored (800) and bases on balls (600). It was a very good year.

To make things worse for the rest of the National League, the Dodgers pitching staff was also outstanding. They had the league's best ERA (3.14) and the most saves (22). The staff was led by another of McPhail's shrewd moves – a pitcher that he picked up from the Phillies by the name of Kirby Higbe. All that Higbe and Wyatt did together was to win twenty-two games each. In addition, Casey won fourteen and Curt Davis chipped in with a 13-7 record. Fitzsimmons, at age thirty-nine, was 6-1, with a magnificent ERA of 2.06 and a shutout under his wide belt. Although Fitzsimmons was knocked out of game three of the World Series when a line drive fractured his kneecap, he continued to pitch sporadically for the Dodgers until 1943, when he became manager of the Phillies.

It was the last year for that Dodgers stalwart, Van Lingle Mungo. He pitched only two innings for the Dodgers and was released. He reappeared as a hurler for the Giants and pitched occasionally during the war years when bodies were scarce. At the end of his long career, he had won 120 games and pitched twenty shutouts.

The Giants had another subpar year. They ended up in fifth place, 25½ games behind the Dodgers. Schumacher, at 12-10, had the most wins on the club. Hubbell was right behind him at 11-9 and Bob Carpenter, in his second year with the Giants, was 11-6. The team's ERA was a mediocre 3.94.

Dick Bartell returned to the Giants and, at age thirty-three, was their only .300 hitter. Ott, of course, led the club in home runs with twenty-seven. Babe Young kept pace again as he finished with twenty-five. The next highest Giant in the home run category had seven. Horace Stoneham, owner of the Giants, had seen enough. He fired Bill Terry and named Mel Ott as player-manager for 1942.

In a year that saw Joe DiMaggio hit in fifty-six consecutive games, and Ted Williams bat .406, the big story in New York was the first meeting ever in a World Series between the Yankees and the Dodgers. The series lived up to expectations in the drama department. One recalls the passed ball by Dodgers catcher, Mickey Owen, that opened the door for a two-out, ninth inning rally by the Yankees in Game Four. A win would have tied the Series at two games apiece. There were many other "could have beens" in the Yankees five-game victory in the Fall classic.

For example, would the Yankees have won Game Three if Fitzsimmons had not had his kneecap fractured by a line drive? "Fat Freddie" had already pitched seven scoreless innings prior to the mishap. Hugh Casey had to be rushed in and was the loser. In fact, Casey was the losing pitcher in three of the Yankees four victories. Owen is always thought of as the goat in Game Four for not stopping the pitch that should have struck out Tommy Henrich and thereby opening the floodgates that led to victory. However, it was still two out and only Tommy Henrich on base. It was Casey who gave up two-out hits to DiMaggio and Keller, walked Dickey and then gave up a double to Joe Gordon that sealed Brooklyn's fate.

Baseball is a strange and often cruel game. Casey had been the premier reliever in the National League that year. He finished with fourteen wins and seven saves during the regular season. Yet, in the World Series, he was battered constantly by the big Yankees bats.

There were some other notable events in 1941. Hank Greenberg, the Detroit Tigers slugger, had been the first Major leaguer to enlist in the armed forces – he had done so at the close of the 1940 season, after Detroit lost to Cincinnati in the World Series. Hugh Mulcahy, a pitcher for the Phillies, had the dubious honor of being the first of many Major Leaguers to be drafted, when his number was called on March 8, 1941. December 7th was still in the future.

This had been the year that the Dodgers became the first team in the Major Leagues to use plastic batting helmets, after both of their young stars, Reese and Reiser, were beaned.

1941 was also the year that baseball said goodbye to one of its all-time greats, when Lou Gehrig died of what would come to be known as "Lou Gehrig disease."

Dodgers		**1941**	**Giants**	
Pete Reiser	.343*	**BA**	Dick Bartell	.303
Dolph Camilli	120*	**RBI**	Babe Young	104
" " " "	34*	**HR**	Mel Ott	27
Kirby Higbe Whit Wyatt	22*	**WINS**	Hal Schumacher	12
Whit Wyatt	2.34	**ERA**	Cliff Melton	3.02
" " "	176	**SO**	" " "	100

* led the National League

1942

Reiser Hits the Wall

July, 1942 was over. Brooklyn was in first place by 10½ games and, despite the war, Dodgers fans were working themselves up to an appropriate frenzy for their first consecutive pennants in the twentieth century, and an anticipated rematch with the hated Yankees. The general feeling in Brooklyn was; "This time, Owen holds on to the third strike and we bury them."

Then the unthinkable happened. St. Louis finished the season with a 43-8 surge that brought them the pennant and the stunned Dodgers fans had to resort to their patented cry: "Wait 'till next year!" There were other reasons for the lost pennant in addition to St. Louis' remarkable streak. Pete Reiser had run into a wall again on July 2nd. He was hitting .390 at the time, but after hitting the wall his average sank eighty points by the end of the season.

The Dodgers were 13½ games ahead of the Cardinals when Reiser hit the unpadded wall and many knowledgeable observers felt that the Cardinals could never have caught Brooklyn if Reiser had remained uninjured. This proved to be an indicator of how Reiser's career would unfold. His propensity for running into walls and total disregard for personal injury led to a diminished career. Reiser eventually appeared in only 861 games – an average of less than eighty-seven games a season – and many of those appearances were made at far less than full strength. Even in the injury-marred season of 1942, he managed to lead the league in stolen bases with twenty. (The Dodgers led the league with seventy-nine.)

Dolf Camilli hit twenty-six homers and drove in 109 runs. Joe Medwick hit .300 but his home run production dropped from eighteen in '41 to only four in 1942. The Dodgers, as a team, hit thirty-nine less home runs than they did in the previous year.

On the mound, Whit Wyatt won nineteen and lost only seven. Larry French was sensational at age thirty-four, with a 15-4 record and an ERA of only 1.82 in 148 innings! He pitched a one-hitter in his last start before going into the navy. This created an oddity as French had the distinction of having led the national league in winning percentage in the last year that he ever pitched in the Major Leagues. In another oddity, French won 197 games in his Major League career without ever winning twenty games in a season.

Kirby Higbe, out of Columbia, South Carolina, won sixteen, as did Curt Davis at age thirty-eight. Davis had a more than respectable 2.36 ERA. Rookie Ed Head won ten games, as did Johnny Allen. Hugh Casey once again led all Major League relievers with thirteen saves, but, despite all of this, the Durocher men ended the season two games out of first place. They had the minor satisfaction of tying the National League record of 104 wins for an also-ran. St. Louis was an incredible 106-48 for the season.

To rub salt in Dodgers fans wounds, the Cardinals took the Yankees four games to one in the World Series – proving to Brooklyn's fans that the Yanks were ready to be beaten. (A more unbiased estimate might have been that the Cardinal pitching was just that good – their staff ERA of 2.55, their eighteen shutouts and 651 strikeouts had led the National League.)

In Mel Ott's first year as their skipper, the Giants made their way back to the first division in 1942. They finished third, although a full eighteen games behind Brooklyn. The Giants led the league in home runs with 109 – the Dodgers had only sixty-two. Johnny Mize, the "big cat" from Demarest, Georgia, had been traded to the Giants from the Cardinals during the off-season. The burly, left-handed slugger found the short right field fence at the Polo Grounds to be friendly. He hit twenty-six home runs, batted .305 and led the National League in RBI's with 110. Mel Ott once again led the league in homers with thirty. He was also walked more than any other National Leaguer once again – 109 times. Ott set a record by drawing one hundred or more bases on balls for seven consecutive seasons.

Unfortunately, Mize was the only Giant to bat .300 and, on the mound, Bill Lohrman won the most games with only thirteen victories. His 13-4 record, and Cliff Melton's 11-5 were bright spots. Despite the fine record, Melton had elbow trouble all year that continued into 1943. A twenty-two-year old named Harry Feldman, who had pitched in just three games in 1941, impressed everyone with a 7-1 record. Ace Adams set a National League record by appearing in sixty-one games. As his 1.84 ERA would indicate, he was an effective relief pitcher.

However, no Giants pitcher struck out more than sixty-one batters and the staff gave up 1,299 hits. By comparison, Dodgers pitchers yielded 1,205 hits and the Cardinals only 1,192. Even fourth-place Cincinnati gave up only 1,213. Having given up 493 walks, as opposed to only 497 strikeouts, the Giants were fortunate to have had the hitting that enabled them to finish third.

Much of the credit must go to Mel Ott who, in addition to thirty homers and 109 walks, led the National League in runs scored with 118. The former, seventeen-year-old phenom was now thirty-three and still carrying the club with his big bat. He would never reach thirty home runs again, but Ott was not through yet by any means.

Dodgers		1942	Giants	
Pete Reiser	.310	**BA**	Johnny Mize	.305
Dolph Camilli	109	**RBI**	" " "	110*
" " " "	26	**HR**	Mel Ott	30*
Whit Wyatt	19	**WINS**	Bill Lohrman	13
Larry French	1.82	**ERA**	" " "	2.56
Kirby Higbe	115	**SO**	Carl Hubbell Cliff Melton	61

* led the National League

1943

At Age 40, King Carl Delivers

Dolf Camilli retired ninety-five games into the season and the Dodgers brought up a twenty-year-old rookie, Howie Schultz, out of St. Paul, Minnesota, to play first base. Poor Branch Rickey had to watch in agony as his new team finished 23½ games back of the Cardinals club that he had put together.

An area that needed improvement immediately was the pitching staff. The Dodgers had the dubious distinction of drawing the most walks (580) and of issuing the most (637). The three "aces," Wyatt, Higbe and Davis turned in a combined record of thirty-seven wins and twenty-eight losses. Bobo Newsom and Ed Head each won nine as the Dodgers finished third – 5½ games behind Cincinnati. Billy Herman continued to deliver. He led the club in batting with a .330 average and drove in 100 runs.

The war effort seemed to affect every club except St. Louis. New stars like a twenty-two year old Stan Musial, arose to replace those lost to the armed forces or to defense work. All Musial did was to lead the National League in batting (.357), triples (20), doubles (48), hits (220), and total bases (347). Not surprisingly, he was the National League's Most Valuable Player and the Cardinals won the pennant by eighteen games over second place Cincinnati..

The third-place Dodgers ERA was the second worst in the league at 3.88. Worst was the Giants at 4.08. Ace Adams outdid himself for the Giants by appearing in seventy games. This time his nine saves were not enough to take the crown as Les Webber of the Dodgers, appearing in only fifty-four games, won it with ten. Webber did have the advantage of a hard-hitting team that often came from behind to win games. Still, Adams, at 11-7, was the only

Giant to win in double figures. Worse yet, was the fact that none of their other starters had even a .500 won-lost percentage. The Giants gave up the most hits in the National League (1,473). By comparison, the Dodgers gave up only 1.230. The Dodgers total happened to be the league's best.

Once again, the Giants led the National League in home runs with eighty-one – Ott led the club with eighteen. (No other Giant hit more than six.) Mickey Witek, the second baseman, was their only .300 hitter (.314). The weak attack and mediocre pitching resulted in, as might be expected, a last-place finish for the Giants. It was only the third time in the century that the Giants had finished last and the first time since 1915.

Still, it was a war year and, with many of the stars gone, anything could happen and results could come from unexpected sources. For example, the Dodgers got some production from draft-exempt, forty-year-old Paul Waner. The future Hall of Famer appeared in eighty-two games and hit .311. Their thirty-one year-old infielder, Arky Vaughan, led the league with thirty-one stolen bases, and Augie Galan drew the most bases-on-balls (103), while leading the club with nine home runs.

The Giants had seven regulars in their thirties. With yet another injury to catcher, Ernie Lombardi, the thirty-seven-year-old Gus Mancuso was pressed into action. In ninety-four games, he hit an anemic .198 – even against wartime pitching! On the other hand, the draft-exempt, age forty Carl Hubbell, appeared in twelve games and won four – although he did have an uncharacteristic ERA of 4.91. More like "King Carl" was his total of thirty-one strikeouts in sixty-six innings.

Most war year fill-ins were just that: bodies that were needed to fill out rosters and keep the game going. One such example was Bobby-Raymond-Franklin Coombs from Goodwins Mills, Maine. The Giants added him to shore up a depleted pitching staff. Coombs had had a "cup of coffee" with the American League's

Philadelphia club in 1933 and then dropped out of sight. He had been twenty-five at the time, appearing in twenty-one games, with a record of 0-1 and an enormous 7.55 ERA. However, in this emergency, the Giants turned to him – at least he had big league experience – and Coombs, now thirty-five, was delighted to comply. He appeared in nine games, was once more 0-1, and had an ERA of 12.94! Clearly, he had not improved with age.

Dodgers		1943	Giants	
Billy Herman	.330	**BA**	Mickey Witek	.314
" " "	100*	**RBI**	Sid Gordon	63
Augie Galan	9	**HR**	Mel Ott	18
Whit Wyatt	14	**WINS**	Ace Adams	11
" " "	2.49	**ERA**	Cliff Melton	3.19
Kirby Higbe	108	**SO**	Ken Chase	86

* led the National League

Despite the efforts of these "senior citizens," the Giants finish out of the first division in 1944. *Left to right*: Joe Medwick, Mel Ott, Phil Weintraub and Ernie Lombardi.

1944

Walker Feasts on Wartime Pitching

In 1944, with so many top players gone, strange things continued to happen. None stranger, however, than the American League's St. Louis Browns winning a pennant – their first in the twentieth century. Of course, the Cardinals, still potent, thanks to Branch Rickey and despite the war, won their third straight National League flag. This time they won by 14½ games over second-place Pittsburgh. They then disposed of the Browns in six games in the World Series. The first, and probably the last, home town World Series ever for the city of St. Louis. (The Browns were moved to Baltimore at the end of the 1953 season.)

Given the fluidity of the available talent pool, and the general uncertainty, it was not surprising to see the Dodgers sink from third to seventh in the league standings, while the Giants moved up to fifth. Both teams were hard pressed to put rosters together.

The Dodgers had only two regulars, Walker and Galan, batting over .290. A low point came in Boston when Jim Tobin not only no-hit them, but hit a home run in a 2-0 victory. The Dodgers demise, however, was mainly in the pitching area. Forty-year-old Curt Davis was 10-11 and was the only Brooklyn pitcher to win in double figures. The team ERA was the worst in the league at 4.68. Coincidentally, the Giants were the only other team with an ERA over 4.00 – theirs was 4.29. The Dodgers pitchers gave up the most walks (660). Hal Gregg, in his second year, helped them to gain that distinction by walking 137 batters in 198 innings. It helped him to achieve an ERA of 5.45. Gregg had a live fastball, but neither he, the catcher, nor the batter ever knew where it was going. Things were so desperate for the Brooklyn pitching staff that Ben Chapman, a lifetime .300 hitter as an outfielder, came back to the

Major Leagues to pitch for Brooklyn at age thirty-five. He had been completely out of baseball for three years. Comparatively speaking, the experiment wasn't that bad. The Nashville, Tennessee native appeared in eleven games, went 5-3, with a 3.42 ERA in seventy-nine innings and embarrassed thirty-seven batters by striking them out.

The Giants pitching staff got a lift from Bill Voiselle. After posting a 1-3 record in his previous two years with the club, the lad from Greenwood, South Carolina suddenly blossomed against the "ersatz" Major Leaguers proliferating throughout baseball during this war year. Voiselle was 21-16, with league leadership in both walks allowed, 118, and strikeouts, 161. Nobody was digging in at the plate against the hard throwing righthander. He had an ERA of 3.02 and started the most games in the National League, forty-one.

Another youngster for the Giants, New York City native Harry Feldman, at the tender age of twenty-four, was 11-13, but no one else on the Giants staff won as many as ten games. Ace Adams did manage, once again, to lead the league in saves with thirteen and in appearances with sixty-five. Adams set a record for leading the National League in pitching appearances over consecutive years: he won in 1942 with sixty-one appearances; in 1943 with seventy and in 1944 with sixty five – a total of 196 games that he pitched in over a three year period often enough to lead the league each time. (Adams appeared in sixty-five games again in 1946, but lost out to Andy Karl of the Phillies, who appeared in sixty-seven.)

Mel Ott, once again, led the club in home runs with twenty-six. The club had two .300 hitters: Joe Medwick, traded to the Giants by Brooklyn the previous year, led the team with a .337 average and Phil Weintraub, from Chicago, who had been in and out of the Major Leagues for six years, returned to play first base and hit .316. He replaced Joe Orengo, who, even against wartime pitching, could manage only a woeful .218 the previous season. Joe went to Detroit for 1944 and closed out his career by hitting .201 for them. His lifetime batting average, over seven years in the Major Leagues, was an anemic .238.

The Giants finished the season thirty-eight games out of first place. The Dodgers were worse, finishing forty-two behind the Cardinals. Dodgers fans did have something to cheer about: the "People's Cherce," Dixie Walker, led the league in hitting with a .357 batting average. He also led the club with thirteen homers.

Dodgers		**1944**	**Giants**	
Dixie Walker	.357*	**BA**	Joe Medwick	.337
Augie Galan	93	**RBI**	Mel Ott	82
Dixie Walker	13	**HR**	" "	26
Curt Davis	10	**WINS**	Bill Voiselle	21
" " "	3.34	**ERA**	" " "	3.02
Hal Gregg	92	**SO**	" " "	161*

* led the National League

1945

Last Year of Wartime Antics

1945 featured a Durocher-driven, surprise third-place finish for Brooklyn. Stan Musial had gone into the army, enabling the Cubs to slip past the Cardinals and win the pennant. In a dramatic World Series, the last of the wartime era, Detroit, led by Hal Newhouser's pitching exploits, beat the Cubs in seven games. It would prove to be the last appearance by the Cubs in a World Series in the twentieth century.

The Dodgers led the league in RBI's with 720 and bases on balls, 629. Eddie Stanky's league-leading 148 walks, still a record for second basemen, helped to pad that statistic. Stanky also scored 128 runs. Known as "The Brat," for his hard-nosed approach to baseball and the way he irritated opponents, Stanky had made the most of his minimal, natural gifts. An ability to foul off pitches, until he got his base on balls, like a modern day Willie Keeler, and a natural toughness, made him a favorite with the former member of the "Gashouse Gang," manager Leo Durocher and Dodgers fans. (When Durocher became manager of the Giants, he made sure to bring Stanky in as a player and to groom him for a managerial job when his playing career was over. Stanky eventually managed for six years in the Major Leagues.)

With four Dodgers batting .300 or more (Rosen .325, Olmo .313, Galan .307 and Walker .300) the club had a potent attack. Walker's 124 RBI's were tops in the Major Leagues. It also helped that four pitchers won ten or more games. Hal Gregg, beginning to mature from being simply a wild fireballer, was 18-13. He was still wild enough to walk a league-leading 120 batters, but he also struck out 139. Only Preacher Roe, who had moved on to Pittsburgh, struck out more (148).

Tom Seats, a Farmington, North Carolina lad, who had been only 2-2 with Detroit's pennant-winning 1940 club, had been out of the Major Leagues ever since. At age thirty-three, Tom resurfaced with Brooklyn and won ten games. When the young arms returned to baseball in 1946, however, Tom was gone for good.

Curt Davis, at age forty-one, still had a good arm. He threw for 150 innings, won ten games and had a respectable 3.24 ERA. Also, a young lefthander named Vic Lombardi, posted a 10-11 record. At only 5'7," Lombardi relied upon guile to get batters out. It worked well enough for the Reedley, California native to last for six years in the big leagues and post fifty victories.

Meanwhile the Giants spent another year in fifth-place. At age thirty-six, Mel Ott again led the club in home runs with twenty-one. It was the culmination of one of the most remarkable streaks in the history of baseball. Beginning with his first full season, in 1928, as a nineteen-year-old, Ott had led the Giants in home runs every year. An incredible, eighteen-year run that even the Babe could not match. (Although the Giants did not offer a Lou Gehrig for Ott to compete with.)

The rest of the Giants did hit enough homers to help the club lead the league in that department with 114 round-trippers. Ott and Lombardi were the only .300 hitters among the regulars. (Lombardi's slowness of foot was legendary. However, he hit the ball so hard that he was always able to post a respectable batting average.) Four pitchers were in double figures for wins: Van Lingle Mungo was 14-7; Bill Voiselle was 14-14; Harry Feldman was 12-13 and Ace Adams, once again the Major League leader in saves, with fifteen, had a record of 11-9. (Actually, he tied in saves with Andy Karl of the Phillies. However, Karl had many more save opportunities with a pitching staff that finished with the worst ERA in the Major Leagues, 4.64.) The Giants ERA was nothing to brag about either. They had an ERA of 4.06. To put the number of saves by Adams and Karl in perspective, only one team in the entire American League had a *total* of sixteen saves for the year.

By the time that the season ended, World War II was over and America could look forward to the return of its heroes and Major League baseball for 1946. It was to prove as exciting a year as the fans could have hoped for.

Dodgers		1945	Giants	
Goody Rosen	.325	BA	Mel Ott	.308
Dixie Walker	124*	RBI	" "	79
Goody Rosen	12	HR	" "	21
Hal Gregg	18	WINS	Van Lingle Mungo Bill Voiselle	14
Curt Davis	3.24	ERA	Van Lingle Mungo	3.20
Hal Gregg	139	SO	Bill Voiselle	115

* led the National League

1946

The Mexican League Takes its Toll

World War II had ended and most of the stars had returned in time for the 1946 season. It should have been a great year for baseball. Unfortunately, a killjoy named Jorge Pasquel had formed a Mexican League and, by flashing enough greenbacks, had enticed a number of "gringos" south of the border. True, the Dodgers lost Mickey Owen and Luis Olmo, but it was the Giants who were truly devastated. Eight of their players, including pitchers like: Ace Adams, Harry Feldman and Sal Maglie were lured away.

For their indiscretion, all of the players who left for the Mexican League were banned from playing in the Major Leagues for five years, but their teams were hurt even more. For example, the Giants finished dead last and the Dodgers might have had a pennant instead of barely losing it to the Cardinals. The two teams finished in a dead heat, but the Cardinals prevailed in the playoffs by sweeping Brooklyn, two games to none. It didn't help the Dodgers that their star, Pete Reiser, broke an ankle three weeks before the playoffs.

On the positive side, the Dodgers still had Dixie Walker. At thirty-five, the veteran right-fielder could still tattoo the right field scoreboard as well as play the caroms when he was in the outfield. He led the club with twenty-nine doubles and 116 RBI's. Dixie's .319 batting average made him the only .300 hitter in the Brooklyn lineup. Despite the injury that limited Reiser to 112 games, Pistol Pete still led the league in stolen bases with thirty-four and set a National League record by stealing home seven times.

Eddie Stanky, the Dodgers pugnacious second baseman, once again led the league in bases-on-balls with 137 and a young outfielder named Carl Furillo awed fans with his powerful throwing arm.   His throws, plus the fact that Furillo hailed from Pennsylvania, soon earned him the nickname: "The Reading Rifle." In his first year as a major leaguer, he hit a respectable .284 and had a slugging average of .400. Furillo would spend his entire fourteen-year career with the Dodgers.

Pitching was the key to Brooklyn's success in 1946. The staff led the National League in strikeouts (647) and saves (28). Five pitchers won ten or more games, with Higbe the leader at 17-8. Higbe had three shutouts and led the club with 134 strikeouts. He was only one behind Johnny Schmitz, the big left-hander of the third-place Cubs, who had 135.   Hugh Casey was still the "fireman." He appeared in forty-six games, even started one, and finished at 11-5 with a dazzling 1.98 ERA. Ed Head celebrated his return from the military by throwing a no-hitter on April 23rd, against Boston, at Ebbets Field. (The author had the thrill of being in the stands on that occasion.)   At age forty-two, Curt Davis appeared in one game, pitched two innings, was clobbered and retired.   It was an unfortunate curtain call to a fine career for "Coonskin," from Greenfield, Missouri. He had spent eleven years in the Major Leagues and won 158 games as against 131 losses. He pitched 2,324 innings and retired with an ERA of 3.42.

The Giants, with Mel Ott still at the helm, tried to regroup without their eight "renegades," but, when big Johnny Mize, who was hitting .337 at the time with twenty-two home runs, broke his hand, the Giants were effectively done for the year. Those twenty-two homers were enough to lead the club.   An elbow injury to catcher Walker Cooper, that cost him half the season, was another crusher. (The front office wasn't thrilled about the injury either. In addition to Cooper's value to the team, the Giants had shelled out $75,000 to the Cardinals for the catcher during the off-season.) No other regular hit .300 but, once again, the short distances down the foul lines at the Polo Grounds enabled the club to lead the league in home runs with 121. The Dodgers finished with eighty-three.

A twenty-six-year-old lefty named Dave Koslo out of Menasha, Wisconsin won the most games for the Giants, (14) who finished thirty-six games out of first place. Koslo also lost more games than any pitcher in the league (nineteen). No other Giants pitcher won more than nine and no one in the regular rotation had a won-lost record above .500.

A wild left-hander named Monte Kennedy, out of Amelia, Virginia, went 9-10, and managed to lead the league in walks with 116. The staff's ERA of 3.92 was the second worst in the National League. Philadelphia saved the Giants that embarrassment by posting a 3.99 ERA. St. Louis led the league in that department with a 3.01 ERA and the Dodgers were right behind them at 3.05.

Vince DiMaggio, Joe's older brother, came over to the Giants in mid-season and, at age thirty-three, batted twenty-five times without a hit. He wisely retired at the end of the season. Vince always had power, and many a general manager hoped that it was in the genes for Vince to emulate Joe, but Vince retired with a .240 career batting average. In his ten-year career, with four other teams, he did smack 125 home runs and had a lifetime slugging average of .413.

Despite all of the Polo Grounders' home runs, the Dodgers scored 701 runs to the Giants 612 and hit 233 doubles to the Giants 176. The Dodgers led the league in triples with sixty-six – the Giants had 37. One bright spot for the Giants was the fielding of their shortstop, Buddy Kerr. He set a Major League record for shortstops by finishing the season with a fielding average of .982.

It was a frustrating season for Mel Ott. Nothing had gone right since the desertions to the Mexican League. Ott was basically a low-key person, but the pressure was always there and revealed itself most dramatically on June 9th, when he became the first manager ever to be ejected from both games of a doubleheader!

Dodgers		1946	Giants	
Dixie Walker	.319	**BA**	Johnny Mize	.337
" " " "	116	**RBI**	" " "	70
Pete Reiser	11	**HR**	" " "	22
Kirby Higbe	17	**WINS**	Dave Koslo	14
Joe Hatten	2.84	**ERA**	Monte Kennedy	3.42
Kirby Higbe	134	**SO**	Dave Koslo	121

The infield that sparked the Dodgers and led to a pennant in 1947
(left to right): Spider Jorgensen, Eddie Stanky, Pee Wee Reese and
Jackie Robinson.

1947

Dodgers "Steal" a Pennant

In 1947, the Giants climbed out of the cellar and finished in the first division. Their fourth-place finish resulted from winning twenty more games than in 1946. Instrumental in their rise was the arrival of a twenty-six-year-old rookie right-hander from Verboort, Oregon named Larry Jansen. He was an immediate star, posting a 21-5 record and leading the pitching staff, not only in wins, but also in ERA (3.16) and strikeouts (104). Left-hander Dave Koslo was 15-10, with a horrible 4.40 ERA, and none of the Giants other hurlers won more than nine games.

The big story of 1947 for the Giants was their home run production. They hit 221, an increase of one hundred from the previous year. Even with Ralph Kiner belting fifty-one and Hank Greenberg hitting twenty-five for the last-place Pirates, the Giants total was the highest in the Major Leagues. A key contributor for the Giants was Johnny Mize, whose fifty-one homers not only equaled Kiner, but set a record for National League first basemen that lasted until 1998!

Willard Marshall, a sweet swinging, left-handed hitter out of Richmond, Virginia, chipped in with thirty-six round trippers; Walker Cooper had thirty-five and four other Giants had ten homers or more. Much of that power was dissipated by a pitching staff that had an ERA of 4.44. Of interest for Giants fans was the arrival of a new "phenom" named Clint Hartung. The muscular, twenty-four-year-old pitcher could really fire the ball. Unfortunately, he learned that Major League batters feast on fast balls and Hartung limped to a 9-7 record with an ERA of 4.57. He was actually a better hitter than a pitcher. Clint belted four homers in ninety-four at bats and

165

had a batting average of .309. In fact, his slugging average of .543 was third best on a club of sluggers.

Still, it was the cross-town rival Dodgers year. Their season started in chaos: their coach, Charlie Dressen, was lured to the Yankees camp by ex-Brooklyn general manager, Larry McPhail. To make matters worse, Leo Durocher, picking up a few extra dollars by writing a column for the Coney Island based "Brooklyn Eagle" newspaper, implied in one of them that McPhail was consorting with gamblers! (Actually, the column was being ghostwritten by Brooklyn's road secretary, Harold Parrott, but nobody cared about that.) Of course, the Yankees were outraged and, when the smoke cleared, Leo, who was already unpopular with the commissioner's office, found himself suspended for the entire season. Burt Shotton became interim manager. McPhail eventually paid the piper too. The conservative Yankees organization fired him at the end of the season for "public brawling!"

However, no amount of front-office turmoil could overshadow the excitement on the field. The Dodgers had brought up the first black ballplayer to appear on a Major League team in the twentieth century and Jackie Robinson was ready both physically and mentally to make it work. Drilled by Branch Rickey to ignore the vicious taunts of players and fans alike, in order to bring about an end to the color barrier in professional baseball, Jackie controlled his fiery, competitive spirit by letting out all of his frustrations upon opposing teams. He was named "Rookie of the Year" as he led the Dodgers to a five-game victory over St. Louis for the National League pennant. Robinson also led the club with 125 runs scored, and his bunting ability and speed enabled him to set a National League record of twenty-eight sacrifice hits by a rookie.

Pete Reiser, the pride of St. Louis, Missouri, managed to run into another wall, get another concussion, and miss over forty games, but he still hit .309 to lead the club. Pete stole fourteen bases, but the daring Robinson took control of that category too by stealing a league-leading twenty-nine. This helped Brooklyn to lead the league in stolen bases with eighty-eight. Robinson alone actually stole as many bases as the entire Giants squad and seven more than the Cubs.

Dixie Walker of Villa Pica, Georgia, was the team's other .300 hitter on a club that had no one reach one hundred RBI's, although Reese did lead the league in runs scored with 132. Reese and Robinson both had twelve homers for a team that hit a grand total of only eighty-three – third lowest in the league. Clearly, the pitching staff was a key element in the team's capture of the National League flag.

That pitching staff still included venerable Hugh Casey, who once again led the league in saves with eighteen. Joe Hatten had another good year, with a 17-8 record. But it was the fresh, young arms that carried the load. Twenty-one-year-old Ralph Branca was 21-12, with a sparkling 2.67 ERA. Vic Lombardi, at twenty-four, won twelve games and Harry Taylor was 10-5. During the season, Brooklyn used nine pitchers in their early twenties, and a nineteen-year-old named Erv Palica.

The Dodgers, who had been Johnny Vander Meer's victims in 1938 for a second consecutive no-hit game, were almost treated in the same manner by another Cincinnati hurler named Ewell Blackwell. Blackwell, with a no-hitter under his belt in his last start, faced the Dodgers in June and had another no-hitter going into the ninth inning. The sidearmer's streak was stopped by one of Brooklyn's weaker bats when Ed Stanky rapped a clean single. Blackwell's streak was no fluke. At one point in the season, the right-hander, known as "the Whip," because of his delivery, won sixteen straight games!

The 1947 World Series between the Dodgers and the Yankees was truly a Fall classic. There was literally no end to the dramatics. After the Yankees easily won the first two games and appeared headed for a sweep, the Dodgers came back to take the next two at Ebbets Field. The Yankees won the fifth game at Ebbets Field and, with the sixth game back at Yankee Stadium, the series appeared to be over – especially with "The Big Chief," Allie Reynolds scheduled to pitch for the Yankees. He had led the Yankees staff with nineteen wins and was an imposing figure on the mound. Surprisingly, the Dodgers knocked Reynolds out in the third inning and scored a shocking 8-6 victory to force a seventh game at their home park.

With the entire borough of Brooklyn in a state of hysteria at the thought that the Dodgers might actually win their first World Series, the Yankees calmly dispatched Brooklyn by a score of 5-2. It was a series that will always be remembered for two dramatic moments. One of these moments focuses upon Cookie Lavagetto pinch-hitting in Game Four against the Yankees Bill Bevens. Bevens, despite wildness, and with two men on base via walks, was one out away from pitching the first no-hit game in World Series history! With both the Dodgers and Yankees fans at Ebbets Field on the edge of their seats, Lavagetto amazed everyone by drilling a pitch off of the scoreboard in right field that not only broke up the no-hitter, but also won the game 3-2 for Brooklyn! Ironically, it was the last game that Bevens ever started in the Major Leagues.

The other moment, which occurred in Game Six, featured a classic image of the usually undemonstrative Joe DiMaggio kicking up dust as he nears second base. The cause of this unusual display by the great Joe D. was an incredible catch by little Al Gionfriddo of a screaming liner hit by Joe that had extra bases written all over it.

This World Series also brought some measure of retribution for Hugh Casey, who struck out Tommy Henrich in the 1941 World Series for what should have been the third out. When Mickey Owen let the ball get away, the Yankees rallied, and poor Casey went from hero to goat. In this series, Casey had two wins and a save. Unfortunately, for the Borough of Brooklyn, although they had come close, that elusive championship had once again evaded them. The familiar cry of "Wait 'till next year" was to be heard yet again.

Dodgers		1947	Giants	
Pete Reiser	.309	**BA**	Walker Cooper	.305
Dixie Walker	94	**RBI**	Johnny Mize	138*
Pee-Wee Reese Jackie Robinson	12	**HR**	" " "	51*
Ralph Branca	21	**WINS**	Larry Jansen	21
" " " "	2.67	**ERA**	" " " "	3.16
" " " "	148	**SO**	" " " "	104

* led the National League

1948

Leo Switches Clubs to ...!

Most pundits predicted that the Dodgers would repeat in 1948; instead, it became known as the year of "Spahn and Sain and two days of rain" in deference to the Braves two aces. Actually, Spahn and Sain won more games between them (42) in 1947, than they did in 1948 (39), but the phrase was catchy and it stuck. Having five regulars hitting over .300 in addition to the best team ERA (3.38) in the league didn't hurt. Behind Spahn and Sain, Boston raced to its first pennant since 1914, when they were known as the "Miracle Braves."

The Dodgers slipped to third place, a game behind St. Louis. Durocher was back from his one-year suspension, but the magic seemed to be gone. Incredibly, when the team fell below .500, at 36-37, Leo jumped to – of all teams – the Giants! The Polo Grounders had finally given up on Mel Ott as a manager. The Giants were 27-38 at the time and had finished in the first division only twice since Ott had taken over the reins in 1942.

Burt Shotton was once again available to lead the Dodgers and the club had a respectable 48-33 record for the rest of the season. A young fireballer named Rex Barney, from Omaha, Nebraska, led the staff, at age twenty-three, with fifteen wins and 138 strikeouts. He endeared himself to Dodgers fans by no-hitting Leo's Giants on September 9th. Also, his four shutouts tied him with the Braves Johnny Sain for the most in the National League. Like most fireballers, however, Barney was wild; he almost led the league in bases on balls, but Johnny Vander Meer, of double no-hit fame, eked him out for the "honor," 124-122.

Ralph Branca was 14-9 and Joe Hatten and Preacher Roe both won in double figures. Roe, whose given name was actually Elwin, would finish his career with Brooklyn in 1954. His duels with Stan Musial, lefty against lefty, thrilled many a fan during his tenure. The veteran, from Ash Flat, Arkansas had a nifty 2.63 ERA to go with his 12-8 record. Hatten was 13-10. The Dodgers led the league in saves again with twenty-two, but an aging Hugh Casey had been displaced as team leader. He posted only four, while Brooklyn born, Hank Behrman, shuttled between Pittsburgh and Brooklyn the year before, and destined to be a Yankee in 1949, led the club with seven saves.

Jackie Robinson had a decent year, batting .296 with twelve home runs and twenty-two stolen bases, but Marv Rackley, a left-handed hitting outfielder was the club's only .300 hitter at .327. Since Rackley had only 281 at-bats, Carl Furillo officially led the team in hitting with a .297. It was the first time that neither the Dodgers nor the Giants could boast having a regular hitting .300 since 1907!

Pete Reiser spent most of the year on the disabled list and Gene Hermanski, a muscular outfielder out of Pittsfield, Massachusetts, led Brooklyn in the power department with fifteen homers. In addition, a rookie named Duke Snider also appeared in fifty-three contests. He hit only .244 in 160 at-bats, but showed some "pop" with a .450 slugging average. The twenty-one-year-old would stick around for a while.

Durocher's Giants were 51-38 after his arrival, but could not make up for their slow start and finished fifth. It was their eighth second division finish in the past nine years. A far cry from the glory days under McGraw. Larry Jansen had another good year. The reliable right-hander posted an 18-12 mark. Sheldon Jones was 16-8 and Ray Poat, a Chicago native, who had voluntarily retired the year before, came back at age thirty-one to win eleven games.

The enigma, Clint Hartung, still trying to fulfill his projected destiny as one of the great ones, tried to concentrate on his pitching in 1948. The result was an 8-8 record in thirty-six games. He had an awful ERA of 4.76. The Giants pitching staff gave up the most hits in the National League (1,425). The Dodgers staff, by comparison, gave up the least – 1,316.

The Giants once again led the National League in home runs with 164. Johnny Mize had forty of them, tying him with Ralph Kiner of Pittsburgh for the league lead. Sid Gordon added thirty. However, no Giants batter hit .300 and the team batting average of .256 was second worst in the league to Cincinnati's .247. On the other hand, the Giants sluggers produced the most runs in the National League, 780. One highlight for the Giants came early in the year when, on May 21st, Lester Layton, a rookie out of Nardin, Oklahoma, became the only Giant ever to pinch hit a home run in his first Major League game. He did it in the ninth inning too! Unfortunately, after his auspicious beginning, Lester hit only .231, with one more home run for the rest of the year and was done as a Major Leaguer.

Incidentally, the Braves "miracle" ended in the World Series as Cleveland's Bob Lemon and company, despite two losses by Bob Feller, disposed of Boston in six games.

Dodgers		1948	Giants	
Carl Furillo	.297	**BA**	Sid Gordon	.299
Jackie Robinson	85	**RBI**	Johnny Mize	125
Gene Hermanski	15	**HR**	Johnny Mize	40*
Rex Barney	15	**WINS**	Larry Jansen	18
Preacher Roe	2.63	**ERA**	Sheldon Jones	3.36
Rex Barney	138	**SO**	Larry Jansen	126

* led the National League

172

1949

Robinson Leads Brooklyn to Pennant

Two exciting pennant races entertained both National and American League fans all year in 1949. In his first year as manager, Casey Stengel earned his nickname as "The 'Ol Perfessor" by juggling an injury-riddled Yankees lineup brilliantly to beat out the Red Sox by one game. (It was the first time in ten tries that Stengel had managed a team to a first division finish, much less a pennant.)

One game was also the winning margin in the National League as the Dodgers outlasted a powerful St. Louis club. The Cardinals suffered losses in four consecutive games in the final week, while the Dodgers survived a nerve-wracking, ten-inning win over Philadelphia on the final day of the season to grab the flag.

Weak pitching was supposedly the Dodgers Achilles Heel, but, despite the lack of a twenty-game winner, the staff, led by a rookie named Don Newcombe (17-8), and veteran Preacher Roe (15-6) had just enough to win it. The Dodgers led the league in shutouts with fifteen, and Newcombe had five of them. For his efforts, big Don was voted "Rookie of the Year." Roe added three shutouts to the total.

No one had any complaints about the Dodgers offense – it was awesome. They led the league in home runs with 152 and in RBI's with 816. Jackie Robinson led the National League with a .342 batting average and had a total of 203 hits. It was the first time that a Brooklyn batter had collected 200 hits in a season since Babe Herman and Johnny Frederick both did it in 1930. Robinson added 124 RBI's and topped off his super season by leading the National League in stolen bases with thirty-seven. It was little wonder that

Robinson was voted the National League's Most Valuable Player. Quite an accomplishment for someone playing in only his third year in the majors.

Pee Wee Reese stole twenty-six bases and led the league in runs scored with 132 (still a record for shortstops). Gil Hodges, switched from catcher to first base, surprised everyone by being a smooth operator in the field. He celebrated his new position by hitting twenty-three home runs, to tie him with the rookie outfielder, Duke Snider. Carl Furillo hit .322 with eighteen homers and Campanella, a rock behind the plate, batted .278 with twenty-two home runs. Robinson and Reese each contributed sixteen round-trippers to the total.

The Dodgers could feature speed as well as power. Their league-leading 117 stolen bases not only was high for both leagues, but was more than the total of all four teams below them in the standings. Second-place St. Louis had seventeen! (a new National League low).

Durocher's Giants quietly finished fifth again. Their top two pitchers, Sheldon Jones and Larry Jansen each won fifteen and the staff ERA was 3.82. The Giants kept hoping that Clint Hartung would someday live up to his advance billing, but Clint had another mediocre season – going 9-11 and suffering another horrible ERA (4.99). Jones, at 15-12, was the only regular hurler on the club with a winning record. Dave Koslo was a ray of sunshine for Durocher. Despite an 11-14 total, Koslo's ERA of 2.50 topped all pitchers in the National League. He became the first pitcher ever to win an ERA title without throwing a shutout!

The offense for the Giants was adequate, although not spectacular – Marshall (.307), Thomson (.309) and Lockman (.301) were their .300 hitters. They did set a modern NL record, which stood until 1999, when they scored in thirteen consecutive innings from July 18-20, but run production was usually scarce (the Giants had a total of 690 RBI's for the year). By comparison, Brooklyn had 816 RBI's. Thomson clouted twenty-seven homers, Gordon had twenty-six and Mize, at age thirty-six, had eighteen. (Mize would be revitalized when Stengel picked him up for the Yankees the following year. He would hit twenty-five homers for Stengel in only ninety games.)

Leo knew that he needed someone to spark his team, but he would have to wait until next year to get him. Eddie Stanky was still a Brave.

After two such exciting pennant races, the World Series was almost anticlimactic – except for Dodgers fans praying for their first championship of the twentieth century. The first two games were pitching duels decided by the same 1-0 scores. Reynolds beat Newcombe in Game 1, but Roe turned the tables on the Yankees and Vic Raschi in Game 2. The hopes of Dodgers fans would, however, be in vain once again. The Yankees stunned them by reeling off three consecutive wins at Ebbets Field, no less, to take the series. The Brooklyn bats that had boomed so loudly all throughout the season produced a sickly .210 batting average against the Yankees staff, and only fourteen runs in five games. Reese's six hits in nineteen at-bats were the Dodgers major offense. Robinson's brilliant season was dampened when he had only three hits in sixteen at-bats. It was, once again, "Wait 'till next year" time in the embattled borough.

Dodgers		1949	Giants	
Jackie Robinson	.342*	**BA**	Bobby Thomson	.309
" " " "	124	**RBI**	" " " "	109
Gil Hodges Duke Snider	23	**HR**	" " " "	27
Don Newcombe	17	**WINS**	Larry Jansen Sheldon Jones	15
Preacher Roe	2.79	**ERA**	Dave Koslo	2.50*
Don Newcombe	149	**SO**	Larry Jansen	113

* led the National League

1950

Stanky Rejoins Durocher

The slow, power-hitting Giants of 1949 were not Durocher's kind of team and, as soon as the season was over, he made his move. He traded sluggers Willard Marshall and Sid Gordon to the Braves for the double play combination of shortstop Alvin Dark and second baseman Eddie Stanky. Stanky was, of course, Leo's kind of ballplayer: a throwback to the Gashouse Gang of Durocher's days in St. Louis.

"The little general," as Stanky was called, celebrated his reunion with Durocher by hitting .300 for the first time in his career. He also led the National League in assists and putouts. The new infield combination was all that the Giants could have hoped for defensively, and Stanky's National League leading 144 walks helped move the Giants to a third-place finish – only three games behind second-place Brooklyn.

A good double-play combination helps make good pitchers better and that was exactly what happened for the Giants. Larry Jansen, with a 19-13 record, led a staff that included five pitchers winning in double figures. Jansen had an excellent 2.71 ERA and Sal Maglie, at age thirty-three back from his suspension for jumping to the Mexican League, was a sensational 18-4. Jim Hearn tied for the National League lead in shutouts with Maglie and Jansen – all three had five! The Giants led the National League in the shutout department with nineteen. Hearn, acquired from the Cardinals early in the season, had a remarkable ERA of only 1.94 and the staff ERA of 2.49 also led the league.

The Giants had picked up Hank Thompson from the St. Louis Browns and he proved to be a valuable acquisition with twenty homers and 91 RBI's. Despite losing Marshall and Gordon, the Giants still had some punch. In addition to Thompson's twenty homers, Bobby Thomson and catcher Wes Westrum both led the club with twenty-three. The Giants tried a youngster named Tookie Gilbert at first base to replace Johnny Mize. Unfortunately, while Mize was helping the Yankees to another championship, Gilbert batted .220 in 113 games. The problem was solved the following year, when Whitey Lockman and his big bat were brought in from the outfield to play first base. Whitey proved surprisingly adept at the position.

Everyone expected the Dodgers powerhouse to repeat in 1950, but it was not to be. The Phillies, forever after to be known as the "Whiz kids," stole the pennant from under the unsuspecting Dodgers noses. The whiz kids made it interesting though. Leading the Dodgers by seven games, with only nine left to play, they managed to lose all but one game of their lead. In fact, the Dodgers had a chance to tie them, head-to-head on the last day of the season and force a playoff.

On that day, Brooklyn's prospects were good. The Phillies were forced to start their ace, Robin Roberts, for the third time in five days (their other ace, Curt Simmons, had been called up for military duty due to the Korean crisis) and their catcher, Andy Seminick was injured. To make things worse, the slumping Phillies had to face a rested Don Newcombe, who had shut them out in their previous meeting. The gutsy Roberts hung in there, however, got out of a bases loaded, one out situation in the bottom of the ninth inning and became the winner when Dick Sisler hit a three-run homer in the tenth. Just as in the previous year's World Series, disaster had struck at Ebbets Field.

It was a great win for Philadelphia which, prior to this season, had finished in the first division of the National League only once since 1917. Except for the last day of the season, Brooklyn had performed well. Newcombe and Roe both won nineteen and Erv Palica was 13-8. However, as in 1949, the Dodgers had been forced to rely upon their powerful bats, as the pitching staff recorded one of the league's worst ERA's, 4.24. Only last place Pittsburgh was worse, with an ERA of 4.96. On a positive note, Brooklyn did lead the league in strikeouts with 772.

If hitting alone could earn a pennant, the Dodgers would have won easily. They led the National League in batting (.272) and slugging average (.444). They hit the most home runs (194) and had the most RBI's 774. Duke Snider led the league with 199 hits and he and Roy Campanella both belted thirty-one homers. Hodges, Snider and Furillo all drove in more than one hundred runs in the losing effort. Hodges also became the last Brooklyn player to hit four home runs in a single game, when he accomplished the feat on August 31st.

In the World Series, the Yankees easily dispatched the upstart Phillies in four games. Their pitchers gave up a total of only five runs – none of them via home runs.

Dodgers		1950	Giants	
Jackie Robinson	.328	**BA**	Eddie Stanky	.300
Gil Hodges	113	**RBI**	Hank Thompson	91
" " "	32	**HR**	Bobby Thomson	25
Don Newcombe Preacher Roe	19	**WINS**	Larry Jansen	19
Preacher Roe	3.30	**ERA**	Jim Hearn	1.94*
Erv Palica	131	**SO**	Larry Jansen	161

* led the National League

1951

Mays Arrives – Giants Triumph

After their disappointing loss to Philadelphia on the last day of the 1950 season, considered a fluke by most Dodgers fans (especially after the Phillies were dispatched in four games by the Yankees in the World Series), the Dodgers looked forward confidently to the 1951 season. With Newcombe, Roe and a host of young arms on the mound, and their powerful attack, how could Brooklyn lose? Certainly, they could never lose a second straight pennant on the last day of the regular season, could they?

Yes, they could and did. They finished the season in a dead heat with the surprising Giants and were forced to play a three-game playoff to decide the pennant. Will anyone ever forget Bobby Thomson's home run to win the third and deciding game? Certainly, Ralph Branca, who threw the pitch heard round the world, never did.

In retrospect, the ending was in no way foreshadowed by the beginning of the season. The Giants started miserably. In fact, they lost their first eleven games, despite their double-play combination of Dark and Stanky. A major reason for many of the losses was Durocher's stubborn, to some, brilliant to others, decision to keep playing his twenty-year-old rookie, Willie Mays, despite the fact that in game after game Willie could not buy a base hit.

Things got so bad that, at one point, Mays begged Durocher to take him out of the lineup. Leo refused. "You're my center fielder," Mays was told and, as we all know, more prophetic words were rarely spoken.

By early August, as everyone expected, the Dodgers were comfortably ahead of the Giants by 13½ games when, suddenly, all of the pieces fell together for the Polo Grounders. The youthful Mays' exuberance, fantastic play and natural gifts began to reveal themselves. He electrified the crowd in Pittsburgh one day with a barehanded catch of a 457-foot drive! His batting finally came around too, as Leo knew it would, and the consistency of Mays' power hitting helped the club to win a remarkable thirty-nine of its last forty-seven games. They started to roll with a sixteen-game winning streak on August 12th and concluded by winning the last seven games of the season.

For Brooklyn, in the immortal words of Yogi Berra, "It was déjà vu all over again." There they were, on the last day of the season, facing the same Philadelphia club that had "stolen" a pennant from them the year before, and needing a win merely to force a playoff with the Giants. Once again, ominously, the game went into extra innings, but this time, in fourteen torturous innings, the Dodgers prevailed. Were the fates going to give them back the pennant that had been snatched from them in 1950?

It appeared that way when, after splitting the first two games, on an overcast day at the Polo Grounds, the Dodgers apparently had the third game won. They led 4-1 going into the last of the ninth inning and their ace, Don Newcombe, was showing little sign of tiring. There was some nervousness when the Giants rallied by scoring a run and putting two men on base, but Ralph Branca was coming in to relieve and the situation should have been well in hand. The rest is history. Thomson hit the second pitch and sent a lazy fly to left field that dropped into the seats. For a moment, there was complete silence at the old Polo Grounds, and then, pandemonium. The Giants had won the pennant and Thomson became an instant celebrity.

This was not a case of an unknown suddenly becoming a hero. Thomson had been a valuable player for Durocher all year, filling in at third base and the outfield whenever needed. The home run was not a fluke either – for the Polo Grounds that is, where fly balls down the foul lines often found the seats – Thomson had led the Giants with thirty-two during the year and had driven in 101 runs. At age thirty-two, Monte Irvin had driven in 121 runs to lead the league. Despite this, and shortstop, Alvin Dark leading the National League in doubles with forty-nine, the Giants had a team batting average of only .260. Only three teams in the league were lower. The Dodgers led the National League in batting with a .275 average.

The Giants had the Rookie of the Year, in Mays, and the Dodgers had the league's Most Valuable Player in Roy Campanella. Campy hit .325, Robinson finished at .338 and Gil Hodges clouted forty home runs. The Dodgers had the desirable combination of power and speed working for them; they led the National League in stolen bases and home runs! Three Dodgers, Hodges, Snider and Campanella, had over one hundred RBI's and they all hit more home runs than the Giants sluggers, with the exception of Thomson.

Mays was the difference. His inspirational influence on the playing field cannot be overestimated and he well deserved to be named Rookie of the Year. However, the Giants could also boast a tandem of pitchers who led the National League in wins – Sal Maglie and Larry Jansen both won twenty-three games. This helped to balance the achievements of Brooklyn's Preacher Roe who, at age thirty-six, had an incredible year with a record of 22-3 and Don Newcombe, who produced a 20-9 record. Newcombe also led the league in strikeouts with 164. The Giants had an ERA of 3.48 to lead the National League; the Dodgers ERA was 3.88. Clearly, the two teams were closely matched in ability and it was perhaps fitting that the championship should be decided on the last pitch of the 1951 season.

Irvin was a great story. When the Columbia, Alabama product joined the Giants in 1950, at age thirty-one, it was only his second year in organized baseball. All he did in the World Series, as a sophomore, was to steal home in the first game and then lead all hitters in the Fall Classic with eleven hits for a sparkling .458 batting average.

His heroics helped the Giants to give the heavily favored Yankees a scare in the World Series, but they finally succumbed in six games. The Yankees, with Lopat, Reynolds and Raschi to throw at the Giants, just had too much pitching. Ironically, the two Giants aces, Maglie and Jansen, did not win a game in the Series.

Still, it was a great year for the Polo Grounders and, to make it almost perfect, their long-time best player, and former manager, Mel Ott, was inducted into the Baseball Hall of Fame that summer. Seven years later, "Master Melvin, " as he was known would be dead.

On the other side of town, the Dodgers had now lost the pennant on the last day of play for two consecutive years. No other team had ever suffered such an experience and the cry of "Wait 'till next year" was beginning to wear thin.

One oddity in the Brooklyn camp could bring a small smile. Brooklyn pitcher, Clem Labine, got three hits all year in fourteen games – they were all home runs!

Dodgers		1951	Giants	
Jackie Robinson	.338	BA	Monte Irvin	.312
Roy Campanella	108	RBI	" " " "	121*
Gil Hodges	40	HR	Bobby Thomson	32
Preacher Roe	22	WINS	Larry Jansen Sal Maglie	23*
" " "	3.03	ERA	Sal Maglie	2.93
Don Newcombe	164*	SO	" " "	146

* led the National League

182

1952

Dodgers Power Brings Pennant, but ...

After two years of painful, last minute disappointments, Brooklyn's loyal fans were finally rewarded with a pennant in 1952. The Dodgers powerful bats just could not be denied any longer. In a reversal of the previous year's chronology, the Giants, who had started with eleven straight losses, in 1951, before righting themselves and taking the pennant in a dramatic playoff, got off to a great start in 1952. They won sixteen of their first eighteen games, then, suddenly, disaster after disaster struck.

Perhaps it was the trade of Durocher's lucky charm, Eddie Stanky, to St. Louis that brought such misfortune. First, the potent bat of Monte Irvin was lost in spring training, when he broke his ankle. As if that wasn't bad enough, the heart of the team, Willie Mays, was drafted. As for the pitching staff, Maglie and Jansen, both came up with back problems. They won only twenty-nine games between them compared to forty-six the year before.

A rookie knuckleballer named Hoyt Wilhelm, joined the club just in time to, at least, help salvage a second-place finish 4½ games behind Brooklyn. Wilhelm led the National League with a 2.43 ERA and a 15-3 record. In another oddity, Wilhelm homered in his first Major League at-bat; then, despite a Major League career which lasted for twenty years and 431 more at-bats, he never hit another one.

Maglie managed to win eighteen games for the Polo Grounders, while losing only eight. He posted a 2.92 ERA when he was able to pitch. Jansen's back troubles led to a so-so 11-11 record, with an ERA of 4.10. Hearn and Koslo stepped up to help fill the gap with fourteen and ten wins respectively.

After his heroics in the 1951 playoffs, Bobby Thomson had a more typical year – a .270 batting average and twenty-four home runs. Although all eight Giants regulars hit at least ten or more homers, Alvin Dark was the only .300 hitter.

The Dodgers got thirty-two home runs from Hodges; Campanella had twenty-two; Snider belted twenty-one; and both Robinson and Andy Pafko had nineteen. Needless to say, Brooklyn once again led the National League in home runs – this time with 153. (They barely beat the Giants, who accumulated 151.) The Dodgers didn't do it all with the bat. They could field too! Their total for the season of only 106 errors was a new National League record. Pee Wee Reese led the Major Leagues in steals with thirty, as did the team, with a total of ninety. Offensively the Dodgers of 1952 had it all.

This time, they excelled on the mound too. The pitching staff once again led in strikeouts with 773, despite losing Don Newcombe to military service. A rookie, Joe Black, led the staff with a 15-4 mark and a National League leading ERA of 2.15. He went on to become the first black pitcher to win a World Series game. Carl Erskine had been 16-12 in 1951. He did much better in 1952, posting a 14-6 record and leading the team in strikeouts with 131. As a bonus, "Oisk" tossed a no-hitter against the Cubs in June. Billy Loes, back from military service, added a 13-8 record with 115 strikeouts. Roe, at age thirty-seven, was a spot starter and sparkled with an 11-2 record. And a rejuvenated Ben Wade, who had languished in the minors since a brief appearance with the Cubs in 1948, won eleven games for Brooklyn and struck out 118!

The Dodgers were hopeful of gaining their first World Series victory of the twentieth century and the fact that their opponents were once again the New York Yankees, made the thought of victory that much sweeter. This Yankees club had lost the great Joe

DiMaggio to retirement at the end of 1951, so they should have been ripe for the pickings. The Series went the full seven games and featured three home runs by a thirty-nine-year-old Johnny Mize for the Yankees. Duke Snider had four for Brooklyn and things looked good for them as they grabbed a three to two lead in games, with the last two (if necessary) to be played at Ebbets Field.

The expected celebration had to be put off one day for the Borough of Brooklyn as Vic Raschi outdueled Billy Loes, 3-2, to force a seventh game. Still, hopes were high for Dodgers fans as Joe Black, who had won the first game of the Series against Allie Reynolds, squared off against the canny left-hander, Ed Lopat.

All of Stengel's moves seemed magical in 1952, but his pitching change in Game Seven was certainly one of the most notable. Allie Reynolds relieved Lopat in the fourth inning when the Dodgers scored their first run. Reynolds gave up another run in the fifth to temporarily tie the score, but Joe Black was touched up for the go-ahead run in the sixth inning and the Yankees went on to win 4-2. It was a reversal of Game One, as Reynolds was the winner this time and Black the loser.

Reynolds and Raschi both had eighteen strikeouts in the Series and picked up all four wins between them. Mantle had ten hits for the Yankees; Snider and Reese had ten hits apiece for the losers. Snider led all hitters in the Fall Classic with four home runs and eight RBI's. The fans were caught up in the melodrama of Gil Hodges' performance in this series. After hitting thirty-two homers, and driving in over one hundred runs during the regular season, the likeable first baseman was looking forward to showing some power against the Yankees. Instead, with all of Brooklyn groaning after each at-bat, Gil went 0-21.

Dodgers		1952	Giants	
Jackie Robinson	.308	**BA**	Al Dark	.301
Gil Hodges	102	**RBI**	Bobby Thomson	108
" " "	32	**HR**	" " " "	24
Joe Black	15	**WINS**	Sal Maglie	18
" "	2.15	**ERA**	Hoyt Wilhelm	2.43*
Carl Erskine	131	**SO**	Sal Maglie	112

* led the National League

1953

Brooklyn Falls Again

To practically no one's surprise, the Yankees and Dodgers repeated their pennant performances of the previous year. Also, to the surprise of only the most optimistic Dodgers fans, the Yankees prevailed in the 1953 World Series by a four games to two margin. Gil Hodges rebounded from his 0-21 performance the previous year by hitting .364 with a home run in a losing cause.

The Dodgers featured their power game during the regular season. They led the National League with 208 home runs: a team batting average of .285; a slugging average of .474 and 887 RBI's. As an indication of the team's ability to score runs almost at will, the Dodgers set a Major League record by winning a game with a last inning home run, an amazing twenty-four times!

This team had speed too; they led the league in stolen bases with ninety. Brooklyn had the most hits (1,529) and scored the most runs (955) in the National League. By comparison, the champion New York Yankees scored 801 runs (to lead the American League) and had 1,420 hits. The Yankees stole only thirty-four bases. On paper, the Dodgers must have looked invincible.

Roy Campanella led the league with 142 RBI's and was voted the National League's Most Valuable Player award for the second time. In addition to his big bat, Campy was noted for the way that he handled pitchers. His forty-one homers was a Major League record for catchers and, with Duke Snider's forty-two, marked the first time in National League history that teammates had hit forty or more home runs in the same season. Snider and Hodges were close behind Campanella in RBI's with 126 and 122 respectively.

Carl Furillo, "The Reading Rifle," led the league in batting with .344. Snider, Robinson, Campanella and Hodges also hit over .300. To cap off his brilliant year, Snider led the league in runs scored (132); total bases (370); slugging average (.627); and runs produced (216). He finished third in hits, with 198, behind Ashburn (205) and Musial (200).

Junior Gilliam was voted the National League Rookie of the Year. He led the league in triples with seventeen and set a league record for bases on balls by a rookie with an even one hundred. The team was clearly awesome at the plate. At one point in the season, they set a record by homering in twenty-four consecutive games! They also tied a record when no less than six regulars scored one hundred or more runs.

It would seem to be an embarrassment of riches for such a powerhouse to have good pitching too, but Brooklyn did. Their staff was tops in both leagues in strikeouts with 817 and it was the sixth consecutive year that they led the National League in that statistic.

Carl Erskine not only turned in a 20-6 won-lost record, for the league's best percentage, but he struck out 187 batters. With all of that power behind them, the Dodgers pitchers could give up runs and expect their team to come back and win – which might explain the staff's poor ERA of 4.10.

The team won a club record 105 games and finished a full thirteen games ahead of second-place Milwaukee. (The Boston Braves had relocated that winter.) In addition to Erskine, Preacher Roe hung around for another year to enjoy all of the run production and, at age thirty-eight, finished with another fine won-lost record of 11-3. Over a three year period, the Preacher, in his late thirties, had compiled a remarkable total of forty-four wins as against only eight losses. When his career ended the following year, Roe was able to retire with a won-lost percentage of .602 – based upon 127 wins and only eighty-four defeats.

The Giants had slipped back to fifth place in 1953. Their team batting average of .271 and slugging average of .422 were certainly respectable. In addition, they could boast of four .300 hitters with Mueller, .333; Irvin, .329; Hank Thompson, .302 and Alvin Dark, .300. They hit 176 home runs and scored 768. Competitive numbers compared to the rest of the National League, with the exception of the Dodgers who, for this year at least, were in a class by themselves.

It was the Giants pitching that failed them. The team's ERA was 4.25 and they led the league in bases on balls with 610. (The Brooklyn staff walked only 509.) Ruben Gomez was the only hurler above .500 at 13-11. Jansen was a shocking 11-16! No one else won even ten games. Jim Hearn was 9-12 and Dave Koslo also lost in double figures at 6-12. Al Corwin was 6-4, but had an inflated ERA of 4.96. Koslo, Hearn and even Maglie and Jansen had ERA's above 4.00.

The pitching was so bad at one point that Alvin Dark came in from shortstop to relieve and, although he gave up onè run in the one inning that he pitched, he did get a save! The Giants kept trying with Tookie Gilbert and he kept doing his best to prove that they shouldn't. He played in forty-four games at first base and hit a resounding .169. Thomson (26) Thompson (24), Dark (23) and Irvin (21) provided home run power, but the woeful pitching and the loss of the team's soul – Willie Mays – all contributed to a lost season. Willie would return in 1954 and so would the Giants – to contention with a vengeance.

A final note on the 1953 World Series. The Dodgers were almost single-handedly done in by Billie Martin. The Yankees second baseman caught fire with twelve hits, to lead all batters. His .500 batting average included a double, two triples and two home runs. It was the fifth consecutive championship for the pinstripers, who overcame the embarrassment of fourteen strikeouts at the hand of Carl Erskine, in game three, to take it all.

Dodgers		1953	Giants	
Carl Furillo	.344*	**BA**	Don Mueller	.333
Roy Campanella	142*	**RBI**	Bobby Thomson	106
Duke Snider	42	**HR**	" " " "	26
Carl Erskine	20	**WINS**	Ruben Gomez	13
Clem Labine	2.78	**ERA**	" " " "	3.40
Carl Erskine	187	**SO**	" " " "	113

* led the National League

The opening day line-up that everyone assumed would carry
Brooklyn to a third consecutive pennant in 1954 – the Giants had
other ideas. *Left to right:* Junior Gilliam, Pee Wee Reese, Duke
Snider, Jackie Robinson, Mgr. Walt Alston, Roy Campanella, Gil
Hodges, Carl Furillo, Billy Cox and Carl Erskine.

1954

Mays Returns – Giants Win!

When the 1954 season began, Yankees and Dodgers fans were confidently looking forward to a third straight meeting between their clubs in the World Series. They were both to be disappointed.

It took an amazing American League record, 111 wins, by Cleveland, to topple the Yankees, who oddly enough had their best year yet under Stengel, with 103 victories! The surprise win by Cleveland ended a five-year reign as world champions by the Bronx Bombers. (Cleveland had won it all in 1948.)

After winning two consecutive pennants, Chuck Dressen, the Dodgers manager, had had the temerity to ask Walter O'Malley (later, to further distinguish himself by becoming the most hated man in the Borough of Brooklyn's history) for a three-year contract! This outrageous request was met by Dressen's immediate termination and the hiring of mild-mannered, and more tractable, Walter Alston. Unlike Dressen, Alston possessed the virtue of understanding that one-year contracts were the norm for managers of the Brooklyn club. He would remain the manager until 1976.

It didn't help Dressen's cause that in 1953 the Dodgers were the first losing team in World Series history to have a team batting average of .300! In fact, five of Brooklyn's regulars hit over .300 in the World Series and Junior Gilliam just missed with a .296. It was, in Dressen's defense, a high scoring Series, with a total of sixty runs crossing the plate in just six games.

Alston, whose nickname was Smokey, when he played for his one Major League year with St. Louis in 1936, actually only appeared in one game, had one at-bat and struck out. He was twenty-four years old at the time.

O'Malley's gamble seemed to backfire, as the Alston-led Dodgers saw their arch-rivals, the Giants, rebound from a mere seventy wins in 1953 to ninety-seven wins and a pennant in 1954. A major reason for the Giants surprising victory was the return from military duty of Willie Mays. The "Say Hey" kid celebrated his return by leading the National League in batting with a .345 percentage and a .667 slugging average. After a slow start in the home run department (he had only ten by the All-Star break,) Mays finished with forty-one round-trippers to lead the club. He also led his teammates with 119 runs scored. Add to this his 195 hits, second only to teammate Don Mueller's league-leading 212, and Mays' impact can begin to be appreciated. The intangibles of his enthusiasm and amazing fielding and base-running skills must also be added to the mix. Mays was chosen as the National League's MVP almost by acclamation..

Mueller's superb year included a batting average of .342 and the distinction of having struck out the least times on the club – only seventeen times out of 619 at-bats! Dark and Thompson had twenty and twenty-six homers respectively, but no other regulars hit .300.

Despite Mays' heroics, the Giants could not have won the flag if their pitching staff had not improved dramatically. After three undistinguished seasons with the Braves, Johnny Antonelli had gone into the service and matured. Brought to the Giants in the trade with Milwaukee that sent the hero of the 1951 playoffs, Bobby Thomson to the Braves, the left-hander was 21-7, the best winning percentage in the league. He also led the league with a sparkling ERA of 2.29 and six shutouts.

Ironically, the Thomson trade became even more one-sided in the Giants favor when Thomson broke his ankle early in the season. This forced the Braves to try a young infielder in the outfield. The experiment worked. The young infielder, turned outfielder, lasted for twenty-three years and hit 755 home runs. Hank Aaron had begun his fabulous career.

The rest of the Giants pitching staff was less outstanding, but had just enough for the pennant-bound Giants to survive. Ruben Gomez won seventeen and lost nine, with a respectable ERA of 2.88. However, his 106 strikeouts were offset by his issuance of a league-leading 109 bases on balls. Maglie won fourteen and lost only six as Leo's "spot" starter. Maglie was now thirty-seven and had thrown far too many pitches in his career to perform in the regular rotation. Hoyt Wilhelm knuckleballed his way to a 12-4 record and thirty-six-year old Marv Grissom, picked up the previous year to bolster a shaky mound crew, was 10-7. The improvement by the staff from a 4.25 ERA in 1953 to a league-leading ERA of 3.09 was, in addition to the return of Mays, the key to the Giants surprising win in 1954.

No one was more surprised than the Dodgers, who finished a full five games back. They wouldn't have been so mystified if they had checked the statistics. Their team batting average was down fifteen points in 1954, and their slugging average was down thirty. Although they still led the National League, they hit twenty-two less home runs (186) too.

Brooklyn's pitching staff led the league in strikeouts for the fourth consecutive year and they boasted four .300 hitters: Snider (.341), Robinson (.311), Reese (.309) and Hodges (.304). Hodges led the league in home runs with forty-two and drove in 130 runs. Brooklyn also had the league's best slugging average (.444) and Snider equaled Hodges RBI feat with 130 of his own. The Dodgers clearly still had explosive power that could erupt at any time. As an example of this, in the eighth inning of one game during the season, they scored twelve runs after two were out and the bases were empty!

However, despite the strikeouts, the Dodgers pitching just did not measure up to the Giants in 1954. Many bemoaned the loss of

Dressen as manager, since he was renowned for his ability to get the most out of his pitching staff. The team ERA went up to 4.31 from 4.10 and even their strikeout total, while tops in the league, was fifty-five less than the year before. Erskine went from a 20-6 record in 1953 to 18-15; Loes won only thirteen; Meyer and Podres each won eleven and Preacher Roe, finally showing his age at thirty-nine, sank from 11-3 in 1953 to 3-4 in this, his final year. A key indicator of the decrease in pitching efficiency might have been the fact that Russ Meyer led all the starters with a 4.00 ERA.

A bright spot on the Brooklyn staff was Jim Hughes. The Chicago native led the Major Leagues in saves with twenty-four. Another youngster, Karl Spooner, out of Oriskany Falls, New York, startled the baseball world by recording fifteen strikeouts in his first Major League game – a record that is yet to be broken. In fact, he pitched shutouts in his first two appearances! After such an auspicious start, it appeared that a new star had burst upon the baseball scene, but it was not to be. Spooner immediately developed a sore arm and never pitched another inning all year. His arm was never really right after that and, after compiling an 8-6 record in 1955, Spooner was finished with baseball. The record will show, however, that Spooner finished the 1954 season with a perfect ERA of 0.00.

As for the World Series, the Indians, fresh from their record-setting season of 111 wins, were huge favorites to beat the Giants. Many experts considered the Giants winning of the pennant to be a fluke. They were proven wrong as, in a tremendous upset, that must have surprised even a hardened veteran like Manager Leo Durocher, the upstart Giants whipped the Indians in four straight games. It was the first sweep of a World Series by a National League team since another surprising club, the "Miracle" Braves, did it in 1914.

The Giants outscored Cleveland 21-9 and held the big Cleveland bats to a .190 batting average. Vic Wertz was the batting star for the Indians, with eight hits in sixteen at bats. Only two other Indians had as many as three. Wertz, of course, will always be remembered for the hit that he didn't get – a 460-foot drive that Willie Mays turned into a highlight film by catching the ball with his back to the plate while running at full speed. In addition, Mays then had the presence of mind to turn and throw, preventing the two baserunners from advancing. It was clearly one of the great catches in World Series history.

To make matters worse, and set the mood for the entire Series, Dusty Rhodes then hit a tenth-inning home run (what pundits called a typical Polo Grounds cheapie) that traveled down the right field line, about 260 feet, and into the stands. Dusty, a little known, thirty-seven-year old, utility outfielder for the Giants, caught the attention of the entire nation as he turned this World Series into his own personal stage. His totally unexpected performance included, in addition to that dramatic, three-run, winning home run in Game One, another pinch-hit homer, seven RBI's and four hits – all in only six official at-bats!

Durocher too, was at his managerial best in the Series. After the exciting win in Game One, Antonelli and Gomez set Cleveland down in Games Two and Three. However, Maglie had pitched eight innings in the opener, so Leo gambled with a twenty-nine-year-old unknown named Don Liddle, out of Mt. Carmel, Illinois, to start Game Four. Liddle had won nine games during the regular season, but had completed only four of his nineteen starts. Fortunately for Liddle, and the Giants, he was treated to a seven run lead by the fifth inning and hung on for a 7-4 win. The shocked Indians had been sent packing in four straight. The National League was pleased. It was the league's first victory in the World Series since the Cardinals had squeaked by the Boston Red Sox in 1946.

Dodgers		1954	Giants	
Duke Snider	.341	**BA**	Willie Mays	.345*
Gil Hodges Duke Snider	130	**RBI**	" " "	110
Gil Hodges	42	**HR**	" " "	41
Carl Erskine	18	**WINS**	Johnny Antonelli	21
Russ Meyer	4.00	**ERA**	" " " "	2.29*
Carl Erskine	166	**SO**	" " " "	152

* led the National League

1955

At Last – Brooklyn Prevails!

1955 will always live in the hearts of true Dodgers fans; it was, of course, the year that their "Bums" finally climbed the mountain and won their first World Series. At last, the plaintive wail of "Wait 'till next year," need be heard no more along Flatbush Avenue.

In an exciting World Series, that was in doubt until the final gut-wrenching out of the seventh game, Brooklyn finally prevailed. To make it even sweeter, if that were possible, the victim was the New York Yankees – their chief tormentor over the years in the Fall Classic.

The Dodgers looked like they were headed for their usual post-season debacle, when they dropped the first two games of the Series at Yankee Stadium. But they rallied to take all three of the games at Ebbets field. When they lost Game Six at Yankee Stadium, however, a chill of foreboding gripped the borough of Brooklyn. Then, to everyone's astonishment, Johnny Podres calmly threw an eight-hit, complete game shutout in Game Seven, and the Dodgers were actually World Champions. Podres had also been the winner in Game Three and, after Game Seven, the youngster from Witherbee, New York was clearly the man of the hour.

To get to the World Series, the Dodgers first had to beat out a Milwaukee Braves team that boasted a powerful attack and solid pitching. Fortunately, for Brooklyn, Campanella was back from a hand injury and the pitching staff responded to his presence with a league-leading 3.68 ERA. Campy's work was recognized by his selection as Most Valuable Player for the third time. He and Yogi

Berra are the only catchers in baseball history to have won the award three times.

Don Newcombe, out of Madison, New Jersey, coming off a disappointing 9-8 record in 1954, responded with a 20-5 won-lost total. Big Don backed up his pitching with his bat – he had forty-two hits in thirty-four games. Clem Labine proved to be a superb relief pitcher. He appeared in a league-leading sixty games, with eleven saves and a record of 13-5. Erskine and Loes added eleven and ten wins respectively.

In addition, a new youngster on the staff by the name of Koufax, set a Major League record by striking out twelve consecutive batters on June 24th. To prove that it was no fluke, the Brooklyn native repeated the feat exactly three months later. The future World Series hero, Podres, had suffered through a mediocre year with a 9-10 record and a 3.96 ERA. All of that would be forgotten in October.

At the plate, Duke Snider had another great year. He led the National League in RBI's with 136 and the club in homers with forty-two. For a power hitter, Campanella could hit for average too. He led the club with a .318 batting average. Furillo, at .314, and Snider, at .309, were the only other .300 hitters for Brooklyn.

While the Dodgers basked in the glory of their most successful season since 1900, last year's champions, the Giants, dropped into third place – a full eighteen and a half games back. Hearn and Antonelli both won fourteen, but each lost sixteen too. Don Liddle, the surprise hero of the fourth game of last year's World Series, had a ten and four record, but a terrible ERA of 4.25. He would be traded to the Cardinals the following season – it would be his last in the Major Leagues.

In an interesting turn of events, Sal "The Barber" Maglie, at 9-5 in midseason, got into an argument with Durocher and found himself traded to Cleveland. He never won a game for them, and in another unusual twist of fate, wound up in Brooklyn the following year. Dodgers fans quickly learned to love their former arch-enemy.

Mays, at .319, and Mueller, at .306, hit over .300, but the Giants seemed to have lost their spark. Their RBI's dwindled from 701 in 1954, to 643 in 1955. Mays alone had twenty-four of the team's thirty-eight stolen bases. No one could blame Mays for the club's drop in the standings. The "Say hey" kid led the Giants in batting, with a .319; in RBI's with 127 and in home runs, fifty-one. He thus became the first Giant to lead the National League in home runs since Johnny Mize tied Ralph Kiner of Pittsburgh in 1948, with forty round-trippers. (The same duo tied in 1947 with fifty-one.) Mays was the first Giant to win the home run title outright, since their legend, Mel Ott, did it in 1942. Ott hit thirty during that war year.

The team's lackluster performance so frustrated Durocher that he quit at the end of the season. The colorful manager did not return to baseball until 1966, when he resurfaced with a dreadful Chicago Cubs team that finished dead last.

Dodgers		1955	Giants	
Roy Campanella	.318	**BA**	Willie Mays	.319
Duke Snider	136*	**RBI**	" " "	127
" " "	42	**HR**	" " "	51*
Don Newcombe	20	**WINS**	Johnny Antonelli Jim Hearn	14
" " "	3.19	**ERA**	Johnny Antonelli	3.33
" " "	143	**SO**	" " " "	143

* led the National League

200

1956

Last Pennant for Brooklyn

Milwaukee made an even more determined run at the pennant in 1956, but the Dodgers squeaked by with a 93-61 record to the Braves 92-62. Actually, Brooklyn trailed the Braves by one game, with only three remaining, but the Braves lost two of their last three, while Brooklyn swept all of their remaining games.

The Dodgers pitching was truly outstanding. Their team earned-run average was 3.57 and they led the league in strikeouts with 772. Clem Labine was one of their key producers; he led the Major Leagues in saves with nineteen. However, the big man was Don Newcombe, who carried the club to its narrow victory with a 27-7 record, 139 strikeouts and five shutouts. He not only was named the National League's Most Valuable Player, but he received the very first Cy Young Award ever presented as the best pitcher in the Major Leagues.

Sal Maglie, who had been traded to Cleveland by the Giants the previous year, came to the Dodgers early in the season and, at age thirty-nine, compiled a 13-5 record with a sparkling 2.87 ERA. The veteran, who was one of the most hated of the Giants when he worked for them, quickly became a favorite at Ebbets Field. With his dark shadow of a beard, and a willingness to brush back any batter reckless enough to claim part of home plate, he had earned the sobriquet, "Sal the Barber." Many a hitter, who had received one of Maglie's "close shaves," would testify that the nickname was an apt one. Maglie threw a no-hitter against the Phils on September 25th; it was a key win, with the pennant race approaching its exciting conclusion. He was even the runner-up to Newcombe in the balloting for the Cy Young Award – not bad for a thirty-nine-year-old.

Carl Erskine, with thirteen wins and Roger Craig with twelve were solid contributors. The staff was bolstered by a nineteen-year-old rookie named Don Drysdale, who won five, and their twenty-year-old lefthander, Sandy Koufax, who was 2-4. Sandy was still wild, but he did flash some promise by striking out thirty batters in fifty-nine innings.

The hitting was, once again, ferocious, but much less so than in the championship year of 1955. The team-batting-average dropped thirteen points to .258; the slugging average was down twenty-nine percentage points and, with 191 home runs, they were down by twenty-two in that department also. Still, they had enough power to take it all. Snider led the league in homers with forty-three, slugging average (.598), and on-base percentage (.402) – complemented by his league-leading ninety-nine bases on balls. Junior Gilliam was the club's only .300 hitter, but Furillo, with twenty-one round-trippers, Hodges, with thirty-two and Campanella with twenty, provided plenty of pop in the lineup.

The Giants had a new look in 1956. The Durocher era had ended and Bill Rigney, a reliable infielder for the Giants from 1945-53, had taken over the reins. The team on the field looked different too. Dark had been traded to the Cardinals; a twenty-two-year-old named Bill White was at first base; Schoendienst was at second, which left only Don Mueller, Mays and Rhodes as remaining regulars.

The changes didn't work and the Giants ended up in fifth place, twenty-six full games behind the Dodgers. No Giants regular hit .300 or equaled the 84 RBI's accumulated by Mays. Mays led the Major Leagues in stolen bases with forty.

Johnny Antonelli returned to top form with a 20-13 record, 145 strikeouts and a fine ERA of 2.86. Unfortunately, no other Giants hurler won more than seven games. The staff ERA was 3.78. They did finish second to the Dodgers in strikeouts with 765, but wildness typified their daily performance. They were next-to-last in the league for giving up bases-on-balls with 551.

After being shocked by the Dodgers in the 1955 World Series, the Yankees were bent upon revenge. In a reversal of the previous year, when the Dodgers lost the first two games and went on to win the Series, the Yankees dropped the first two at Ebbets Field. This was not to faze the pinstripers, as they evened the Series and then took a three to two lead behind Don Larsen in a game that will always be remembered as a classic World Series encounter.

Opposing Larsen on the mound that day was the venerable ace, Sal Maglie, who had already beaten the Yankees in Game One. Larsen, on the other had, had been knocked out in the second inning of Game Two. The "smart" money had to be on Maglie. Maglie did come through with a brilliant five-hitter, giving up only two runs, but Larsen was untouchable and pitched the first "perfect game" ever in World Series history.

Undaunted, the Dodgers, behind Clem Labine's shutout pitching, beat the Yankees 1-0 to force a seventh game between the two clubs for the second straight year. Once again, the Dodgers chances looked good. They had been forced to win the seventh game at Yankee Stadium in 1955; this game would be at cozy Ebbets Field. To make it even better, a rested Don Newcombe was ready to go.

With their backs to the wall, in unfriendly Ebbets Field, the Yankees crushed the Dodgers and their fans with a resounding 9-0 win to take the championship. Casey Stengel had once again gambled, this time with his twenty-two-year-old righthander, Johnny Kucks, and the resulting shutout win added to Stengel's growing reputation as the "Ol' Perfessor." Yogi Berra was the batting star of the Series with three home runs and ten RBI's. Hodges was the only .300 hitter of the Brooklyn regulars, and no

Dodgers hit more than one home run in the Series. Thus ended the last World Series for a Dodgers team that made its home in Brooklyn.

Dodgers	1956	Giants	
Jim Gilliam	.300	**BA**	Willie Mays	.296
Duke Snider	101	**RBI**	" " "	84
" " "	43*	**HR**	" " "	36
Don Newcombe	27*	**WINS**	Johnny Antonelli	20
Sal Maglie	2.87	**ERA**	" " " "	2.86
Don Newcombe	139	**SO**	" " " "	145

* led the National League

1957

California, Here We Come

Johnny Podres, the hero of the seventh game of the Dodgers only World Series triumph, was back from the navy in 1957 and he delivered a league-leading ERA of 2.66. Drysdale won seventeen games and Podres twelve, but Newcombe had another off year – finishing with a record of 11-12. Brooklyn slumped to third place, behind pennant-winning Milwaukee, which went on to win another exciting seventh game of a World Series to defeat the Yankees and become World Champions.

The aging Dodgers, with rumors of their imminent departure to warmer climes swirling about their heads all season, and all of Brooklyn in an uproar over the mere thought, had little to brag about. Carl Furillo hit .306 and Snider had another big year – forty home runs and ninety-two RBI's. On the debit side, he also led the league by striking out 104 times.

With the threat of being traded to the Giants looming over him, Jackie Robinson chose to retire instead. Gil Hodges, the catcher converted to first base, won the first Gold Glove award ever. On a lesser note, Reese slumped to a .224 batting average and a terrible slugging average of .248. Snider's slugging average was a hefty .587, while Mays led the league with a .626!

The Dodgers home run production slipped to 147 – fifty-two less than the Braves – and they struck out one hundred times more than in 1956. Their pitching staff did, however, produce twice the shutouts of the Braves (18-9,) with Podres collecting six of them and Newcombe and Drysdale four each.

The Giants, too, were caught up in all of the talk about relocating. They also seemed to be sleepwalking much of the time and ended up a lackluster sixth-place club. They finished a full twenty-six games behind Milwaukee.

Willie Mays seemed to be the only Giant unaffected by the impending upheaval. He led the National League in slugging average (626); stolen bases (38); triples (20); and posted a batting average of .333 with 195 hits. With Willie flying around the bases and chasing down fly balls in the gloomy caverns of the Polo Grounds center field, a memory was created for Giants fans to cherish in the dark days ahead.

No Giants player, other than Mays, hit over .300. The usually reliable Don Mueller had his second consecutive sub-par year – hitting only .258 in 135 games. The Giants traded him to the Chicago White Sox at the end of the season, where he floundered as a part-time performer. The pitching was awful too. The staff had a team ERA of 4.01 (compared to Brooklyn's 3.35) and they had the second worst total of strikeouts in the league – 701. The Dodgers once again led the league in that department with 891. Only Ruben Gomez and Johnny Antonelli with records of (15-13) and (12-18) respectively, won more than nine games. If not for the exceptional relief work of Marv Grissom, who posted twenty-four saves, this last year in the "Big Apple" could have seen the Giants finish in the cellar!

Both the last game between the Dodgers and the Giants at Ebbets Field, which occurred on September 1st, and their last encounter at the Polo Grounds, were won by the Giants. On September, 22nd, the last home run by a Dodger at Ebbets Field was stroked by Duke Snider – his second of the day – against the Phillies. Two days later, on September 24, 1957, the last game ever at Ebbets Field was played between Brooklyn and Pittsburgh, before a "crowd" of 6,702. The Dodgers beat Danny McDevitt, 3-0.

The "honor" of being the last Dodger to bat at the cozy, old ballpark fell to Gil Hodges – perhaps, appropriately, he struck out. On February 23, 1960, the first two-ton ball crushed the visiting dugout to begin the construction of the housing project that was to be built upon what many considered to be "hallowed ground." Due to someone's misguided view of nostalgia, the same wrecking ball was used on April 10, 1964 to knock down the Polo Grounds.

In their last game of the season, on September 29th, the Dodgers beat the Phillies in Philadelphia before less than 10,000. It was ironic that more fans showed up in Philadelphia to see Brooklyn's last game than did so at Ebbets Field for the final home contest. The game itself, meaningless in the league standings, was completed in workmanlike fashion, in less than two hours. That same Sunday, the Giants lost 9-1 to Pittsburgh. Dusty Rhodes, the hero of the 1954 World Series made the last out. Dusty was out of the Major Leagues in 1958, was used briefly as pinch-hitter for the now San Francisco Giants in 1959, batted .188, and quietly retired.

On October 8, 1957, to the surprise of no one, the official announcement was made that the Dodgers were moving to Los Angeles. New York City's gloom became complete when the Yankees fell to the Milwaukee Braves in seven games in the World Series. Said one insightful sportswriter: "It was probably a good thing that the Yankees didn't win the World Series. The city was in no mood for a celebration that included the traditional victory parade."

Both the Dodgers and Giants brass explained that the outmoded parks and inadequate parking facilities were the reasons for the move. Many saw Horace Stoneham, the owner of the Giants, as an unwitting dupe for the greed of the Dodgers' Walter O'Malley who could not go to California alone. That was nonsense. The apparently unsolvable parking problems surrounding the Polo Grounds, increased crime and, most importantly, decreased revenues, dictated the move. Unfortunately for Stoneham, and the

Giants, they never reaped the financial bonanza in San Francisco that the Dodgers enjoyed in Southern California.

In any case, the Dodgers and the Giants were gone and the loyal fans who had loved, and rooted for them for so many years, were left with the empty feeling that accompanies the death of someone close. For, make no mistake, these teams were loved with a passion – and everyone knew that nothing could replace the emotion that this long-time rivalry brought to the Big Apple.

For those of us fortunate enough to have experienced the joy and despair of watching the two teams annual fortunes rise and fall, it is easy to be bitter about their loss. That, however, is self-defeating. Let us rather treasure what we had, and be thankful for the priceless memories that they have left with us. I, for one, will always cherish mine.

Dodgers		1957	Giants	
Carl Furillo	.306	**BA**	Willie Mays	.333
Gil Hodges	98	**RBI**	" " "	97
Duke Snider	40	**HR**	" " "	35
Don Drysdale	17	**WINS**	Ruben Gomez	15
Johnny Podres	2.66*	**ERA**	Curt Barclay	3.44
Don Drysdale	148	**SO**	Johnny Antonelli	114

* led the National League

Extra Innings

Durocher vs McGraw

How do we even begin to compare the feisty Leo Durocher, with the man that no less a personage than Connie Mack glorified by saying: "There has been only one manager and his name is McGraw." John McGraw managed the Giants for thirty-three years. His teams compiled a winning percentage of .589, finished in the first division twenty-eight of those thirty-three years and won ten pennants.

Durocher managed for twenty-four years. His teams compiled a winning percentage of .540, won three pennants and finished in the first division for twenty-one of those twenty-four years. His first division percentage was .920; McGraw's was .849. McGraw finished last three times, Durocher, only once.

McGraw's clubs played in nine World Series. They won three times and lost six others. Their won-lost record in games was 26-28, a .481 won-lost percentage. Durocher lost two of the three World Series that his team participated in. In games, they won seven and lost eight – a .467 percentage.

Comparing the two men at the most equitable ages, thirty-four to forty-three, we see that Durocher's teams were 740-566 in wins and losses for that period; McGraw's were 905-623, (of course, McGraw had Christy Mathewson for 369 of those victories!)

As Major League performers, the edge must go to McGraw. Many fans do not realize that McGraw was a talented infielder, who retired with an impressive lifetime batting average of .334. Playing in the dead ball era, the left-handed hitting McGraw even managed thirteen home runs.

Durocher, on the other hand, while known for his slick fielding and leadership on the field, retired with a lifetime batting average of .247. The only real resemblance between these two may be that they were both fiery competitors who managed the Giants. Perhaps we can agree though that either would have welcomed the other to play for their team.

Vance vs Mathewson

How does one compare Dazzy Vance, or any hurler, to Christy Mathewson? Matty dominated his era as no pitcher, with the possible exception of Walter Johnson, has ever done. From 1900 to 1916, Mathewson started 552 games and completed 435 of them. He won 373 games and lost only 188, for the best ever, won-lost percentage in National League history of .665. Four times he led the league in wins and still holds the record for leading the Major Leagues in shutouts on four different occasions. From 1901 to 1915, he won twenty or more games thirteen times! Along the way, he led the National League in ERA and strikeouts five times (striking out a total of 2,502 batters); he is third highest in all-time career shutouts with eighty; only Grover Cleveland Alexander (99) and Walter Johnson (112) had more. Mathewson was fifth, all-time, with a lifetime ERA of 2.13 and even had twenty-seven saves to his credit.

Against this, Dazzy Vance had a lifetime ERA of 3.24, started 347 games and completed 216 of them. He won 197 and lost 140. He had a total of 2,045 strikeouts and thirty shutouts. He did lead the National League in wins twice, ERA three times, strikeouts seven consecutive times and shutouts four times.

While Vance's statistics are impressive, Mathewson wins hands-down, unless we consider some other factors. Mathewson joined the Giants at age twenty – Vance became a Dodger at age thirty-one. Matty was only effective until age thirty-three; by age thirty-four, he had slipped to being only an eight game winner. At age thirty-five, he won only three games and was, effectively, done as a pitcher.

Vance, on the other hand, led the National League in wins at ages thirty-three and thirty-four. He led the league in ERA at ages thirty-three, thirty-seven and thirty-nine! At age thirty-eight, he still was striking out enough batters to place third in the National League in that statistic. Even at age thirty-nine, he struck out 173 batters and he whiffed 150 at age forty! Unbelievably, at age forty-one, Vance was still strong enough to strike out 103. After age thirty-one, Mathewson never struck out 100 batters in a season.

We might also consider the two teams that these worthies toiled for. From 1901-1916, the Giants of Christy Mathewson won five pennants and were only in the second division three times. During Vance's tenure with Brooklyn, which encompassed the years, 1922-1932, the team was in sixth place, seven times! They were second on one occasion, third on another and fourth twice. Hardly indicative of a powerful club. The Giants of Mathewson's era were the standard, under John McGraw, that all of the National League clubs sought to emulate. The Dodgers were considered league doormats when Vance pitched for them.

Still, there was only one Christy Mathewson. Vance's success as an older player can certainly not diminish Mathewson's undisputed greatness. However, as a senior, and a late bloomer, Vance does deserve recognition. At age thirty-one through age forty, the National League never saw anyone better. He matured like fine wine and we should salute his accomplishment.

Ott vs Snider

Mel Ott had an extensive career at the Polo Grounds, beginning, at age seventeen, in 1926. To make any comparison fair, including this one with Duke Snider of the Dodgers, I will be using the years for both stars when they performed from ages twenty-two to age thirty.

Despite Ott's five-year head start against National League pitching, at age twenty-two both he and Snider had identical batting averages of .292. Ott hit six more home runs that year and had nine more RBI's. Snider had more hits (161-145).

At ages 23-30, Ott led the National League in home runs five times – Snider accomplished the feat only once. One should take into consideration, however, the fact that Snider had some tough competition in that department – Ralph Kiner, Ted Kluzewski, Eddie Matthews, and Hank Aaron, to name a few. Let us also not forget Willie Mays, who belted fifty-one homers in 1955. Perhaps the major consideration should be the scoreboard that towered in Ebbets Field to taunt left-handed hitters, like Snider, while Ott enjoyed the luxury of the short right-field porch in the Polo Grounds.

Snider led the National League in slugging average twice, Ott did it once. Snider led in hits with 199, at age twenty-three, and had 198 hits in two other seasons. Ott reached 190 hits only twice in his career, 191 and 190, to be exact. However, Ott was a clear winner in comparison of RBI's over this ten-year period.

Most fans would concede that Snider's great defensive skills in center field for the Dodgers give him a clear advantage in the fielding department. A look at their comparative lifetime slugging averages is also revealing. Over twenty-two seasons, Ott's slugging average was .533. In eighteen seasons, Snider's slugging average was .540.

Mel Ott's greatness is self-evident and his extended dominance of his peers makes him an undisputed champion of champions. Still, head-to-head, at comparable ages, Snider tends to hold his own.

And Snider vs Mays

You may well ask for a comparison of Snider with a more contemporary peer – Willie Mays. Below is a comparison of their achievements for the last four years that their teams were in New York. (Mays returned from military service in 1954 to lead the Giants to the pennant.)

		Mays	Snider
1954	Batting Average	.345*	.341
	RBI's	110	130
	Home Runs	41	40
1955	Batting Average	.319	.309
	RBI's	127	136*
	Home Runs	51*	42
1956	Batting Average	.296	.292
	RBI's	84	101
	Home Runs	36	43*
1957	Batting Average	.333	.274
	RBI's	97	92
	Home Runs	35	40
Totals	Batting Average	.323	.304
	RBI's	418	459
	Home Runs	163	165

* led the National League

213

For the Record

First Division Finishes

From 1900-1938, the Dodgers were in the first division only ten times; the Giants finished in the first division thirty-three times during the same period. However, from 1939-1957, the Dodgers were in the First Division eighteen times to the Giants total of only seven.

Pennants

From 1900-1957, the Dodgers won ten pennants; the Giants won fifteen. The Dodgers were in the First Division twenty-eight times; the Giants were in the First Division forty times. The Dodgers finished last just once during that period; the Giants finished last five times.

Individual Accomplishments

Some interesting individual accomplishments not mentioned in the text include Jake Daubert leading the Dodgers in batting from 1911-1916, averaging .319 during that stretch. Zack Wheat also led the team for six years, although not consecutively. He led the club in 1910, 1917, 1918, 1920, 1922 and 1924, averaging .328 during those years.

Bill Terry led the Giants from 1929-1935, averaging .355 during the period. Mel Ott led the club in home runs for an amazing consecutive run of eighteen years (1928-1945). During that stretch, he led the National League six times. He also led the club in RBI's eleven times – ten of them consecutive: 1929-1938!

Head-to-Head Competition

Over the years, 1900-1957, the Dodgers leading batter hit for a higher average than the Giants leading batter, thirty-two times. The Giants leading batter hit higher than his Dodgers counterpart, twenty-six times.

In RBI's, the Dodgers leading RBI producer was higher than the Giants top RBI man, twenty-three times; the Giants RBI man led on thirty-three occasions. There were two ties.

Giants sluggers led the Dodgers leading home run hitter thirty-two times, to the Dodgers twenty-three. There were three ties.

As for pitching honors, despite Christy Mathewson, a Dodgers pitcher won more games than the leading Giants pitcher, twenty-eight times; the Giants were close with twenty-seven top marks. There were three ties. As might be expected, with Mathewson and Hubbell in their history, the Giants led in the ERA department, thirty-three times to the Dodgers, twenty-five. The Dodgers, however, had the individual leader in strikeouts, thirty-four times, to the Giants twenty-three – with one tie.

Baseball can be a game of streaks. The Dodgers won seven of their total of ten pennants between 1941 and 1956. The Giants, on the other hand, won ten of their fifteen pennants in the years from 1904-1924.

National League Standing (1900 – 1957)

	Dodgers	Giants		Dodgers	Giants
1900	1	8	1930	4	3
1901	3	7	1931	4	2
1902	2	8	1932	3	6
1903	5	2	1933	6	1
1904	6	1	1934	6	2
1905	8	1	1935	5	3
1906	5	2	1936	7	1
1907	5	4	1937	6	1
1908	7	2	1938	7	3
1909	6	3	1939	3	5
1910	6	2	1940	2	6
1911	7	1	1941	1	5
1912	7	1	1942	2	3
1913	6	1	1943	3	8
1914	5	2	1944	5	7
1915	3	8	1945	3	5
1916	1	4	1946	2	8
1917	7	1	1947	1	4
1918	5	2	1948	3	5
1919	5	2	1949	1	5
1920	1	2	1950	2	3
1921	5	1	1951	2	1
1922	6	1	1952	1	2
1923	6	1	1953	1	5
1924	2	1	1954	2	1
1925	6	2	1955	1	3
1926	6	5	1956	1	6
1927	6	3	1957	3	6
1928	6	2			
1929	6	3			

A Final Word

Clearly there were times when one of these storied franchises dominated the other. Yet throughout the dead ball era, two world wars and the post-war years, one theme remained constant – the bitter, always exciting rivalry between the two clubs.

Did we answer the question as to who was better? Of course not. Hopefully, we did provide some material that Dodgers and Giants fans can use to prove the validity of their own claims beyond a doubt.

We close with one wish: *May the debate never end.*

Index

A

Aaron, Hank, 194, 212
Adams, Ace, 149, 150, 152, 155, 158, 159, 160
Alexander, Grover Cleveland, 59, 210
Alexander, Peter, 116
Allen, Johnny, 148
Alperman, Whitey, 30
Alston, Walter, 191, 192, 193
Ames, Red, 28, 35
Anderson, Fred, 63, 65
Antonelli, Johnny, 193, 196, 197, 199, 200, 202, 204, 206, 208
Ashburn, Richie, 188
Atchison, Raleigh, 54

B

Babick, Johnny, 123
Bagby, Jim, 74
Baker, Home Run, 43
Bancroft, Dave, 76, 79, 82, 102, 107
Barclay, Curt, 208
Barnes, Jesse, 71, 74, 75, 78, 79, 98
Barnes, Virgil, 89, 92, 95, 97, 98
Barney, Rex, 170, 172
Baronn, Red, 103
Bartell, Dick, 129, 135, 144, 146
Batch, Heinie, 24, 25
Beck, Boom Boom, 118
Behrman, Hank, 171
Bell, George, 36, 37, 39
Bell, Hi, 113
Benge, Ray, 118, 119
Bentley, Jack, 85, 86, 89
Benton, Larry, 98, 101, 103, 105
Benton, Rube, 60, 61, 63
Beres, Ray, 130

Berg, Moe, 86
Bergen, Bill, 36
Berger, Wally, 122
Berra, Yogi, 180, 199, 203
Bevens, Bill, 168
Bissonette, Del, 102, 103, 107
Black, Joe, 184, 185, 186
Blackwell, Ewell, 167
Bonura, Zeke, 138, 139
Bordagray, Frenchy, 126
Bottomley, Jim, 88
Boyle, Buzz, 119
Branca, Ralph, 167, 169, 171, 179, 180
Brandt, Ed, 127
Bresnehan, Roger, 15, 18, 19
Brodie, Steve, 17
Brown, Three Finger, 32
Brush, John T., 18, 21
Bucher, Jim, 124
Burns, George, 54, 55, 63, 69, 70, 74, 77
Butcher, Max, 130, 131

C

Cadore, Leon, 71, 77
Camilli, Dolf, 133, 136, 138, 139, 141, 142, 143, 146, 147, 149, 150
Camnitz, Howie, 35
Campanella, Roy, 174, 178, 181, 182, 184, 187, 188, 190, 191, 198, 199, 200, 202
Carey, Max, 98, 102, 113, 118
Carleton, Tex, 140
Carpenter, Bob, 144
Carrick, Bill, 9, 10, 11
Carroll, Ownie, 118
Casey, Hugh, 137, 139, 141, 144, 145, 148, 161, 167, 168, 171

219

Castleman, Slick, 122, 123, 129
Causey, Red, 67
Chance, Frank, 27, 28, 32, 49
Chapman, Ben, 154, 155
Chapman, Ray, 72, 73
Chase, Hal, 72
Chase, Ken, 152
Cheney, Larry, 61
Clark, Watty, 105, 106, 110, 112, 114, 115, 123, 124
Cobb, Ty, 35, 42, 67, 70
Cochran, Mickey, 120
Coffman, Dick, 135
Cohen, Andy, 102, 104
Collins, Ripper, 120
Coombs, Bobby, 151, 152
Cooper, Walker, 87, 161, 165, 169
Corwin, Al, 189
Coscorart, Pete, 138
Coulson, Bob, 41
Cox, Billy, 191
Craig, Roger, 202
Cravath, Garvey, 63
Cronin, Jack, 22
Cronin, Joe, 120
Cuccinello, Tony, 114, 118, 121
Cutshaw, George, 51, 62
Cy Young Award, 134, 201, 202

D

Dahlen, Bill, 15, 17, 21, 22, 25, 39
Dalton, Jack, 54
Danning, Harry, 135, 139, 142
Dark, Alvin, 176, 179, 181, 184, 186, 189, 193, 202
Daubert, Jake, 40, 41, 44, 45, 46, 47, 49, 51, 54, 55, 57, 59, 61, 62, 64, 68, 88, 214
Davis, Curt, 141, 144, 148, 150, 154, 156, 158, 159, 161
Davis, George, 13, 14
Dean, Dizzy, 117, 120
Dean, Paul, 120
DeBerry, Hank, 80
Decauter, Art, 86
Dell, Wheezer, 57

Demaree, Frank, 135, 139, 142
Devlin, Art, 23, 28
Devore, Jack, 39
Dickey, Bill, 145
DiMaggio, Joe, 145, 168, 185
DiMaggio, Vince, 162
Dolan, Mickey, 68
Donlin, Mike, 23, 25, 29, 33, 34
Donovan, Wild Bill, 12, 13, 14, 15, 17
Douglas, Phil, 74, 79
Doyle, Jack, 10, 19
Doyle, Larry, 36, 37, 40, 42, 44, 45, 51, 56, 57, 60, 74
Dressen, Charlie, 166, 192, 195
Drysdale, Don, 202, 205, 208
Durocher, Leo, 7, 120, 123, 130, 137, 138, 141, 148, 157, 166, 170, 171, 174, 175, 176, 179, 180, 183, 194, 195, 196, 199, 200, 202, 209, 210

E

Eason, Mal, 26
Ebbets, Charlie, 9
Ehrhardt, Rube, 91
Eisenstat, Harry, 124
Erskine, Carl, 184, 186, 188, 190, 191, 195, 197, 199, 202
Erwin, Tex, 44
Evers, Johnny, 28, 32, 49

F

Feldman, Harry, 149, 155, 158, 160
Feller, Bob, 172
Fitzsimmons, Freddie, 2, 94, 95, 97, 101, 105, 109, 111, 112, 113, 117, 120, 133, 136, 140, 142, 144, 145
Fletcher, Art, 55, 57
Fournier, Jack, 86, 88, 89, 91, 92, 95
Foxx, Jimmie, 120
Frankhouse, Fred, 126, 130
Frederick, Johnny, 105, 106, 107, 115, 117, 118, 173

220

Freedman, Andrew, 17
French, Larry, 148, 149
Frey, Lonny, 119, 124
Frisch, Frankie, 76, 78, 80, 82, 84, 86, 90, 92, 93, 94, 99, 110, 120
Furillo, Carl, 161, 171, 172, 174, 178, 188, 190, 191, 199, 202, 205, 208

G

Galan, Augie, 143, 151, 152, 154, 156, 157
Ganzel, John, 13, 14
Garvin, Ned, 18, 19, 22
Gehrig, Lou, 94, 97, 120, 130, 146, 158
Gehringer, Charley, 120
Gessler, Doc, 21, 22
Gilbert, Tookie, 177, 189
Gilbert, Wally, 114
Gilliam, Junior, 188, 191, 192, 202, 204
Gionfriddo, Al, 168
Gomez, Ruben, 189, 190, 194, 196, 206, 208
Gonzalez, Mike, 70
Gordon, Joe, 145
Gordon, Sid, 152, 172, 175, 176, 177
Gowdy, Hank, 66
Greenberg, Hank, 120, 145, 165
Gregg, Hal, 154, 156, 157, 159
Griffith, Tommy, 71, 80
Grimes, Burleigh, 68, 69, 73, 74, 75, 77, 78, 80, 85, 86, 88, 91, 95, 96, 97, 100, 130, 134
Grissom, Marv, 194, 206
Groh, Heinie, 79, 80, 82
Gumbert, Harry, 129, 134, 136, 138, 139, 141

H

Hafey, Chick, 111
Hamlin, Luke, 130, 131, 133, 136, 137, 139

Hanlon, Ned, 9, 10, 12
Harper, George, 97
Hart, Jim, 43
Hartung, Clint, 165, 172, 174
Hassett, Buddie, 126, 127, 130
Hatten, Joe, 163, 167, 171
Hawley, Pink, 10, 11
Head, Ed, 148, 150, 161
Hearn, Jim, 176, 178, 184, 189, 199, 200
Hendrick, Harvey, 98, 100, 102
Henrich, Tommy, 145, 168
Herman, Babe, 94, 95, 98, 99, 100, 102, 103, 105, 106, 107, 109, 110, 112, 114, 173
Herman, Billy, 143, 150, 152
Hermanski, Gene, 171, 172
Hershberger, Willard, 140
Herzog, Buck, 46
Hickman, Jim, 64, 65
Hickman, Piano Legs, 10, 11
Higbe, Kirby, 144, 146, 148, 149, 150, 152, 161, 163
Hodges, Gil, 174, 175, 178, 181, 182, 184, 185, 186, 187, 188, 191, 194, 197, 202, 203, 205, 207, 208
Hogan, Shanty, 99, 105, 108, 111
Hooper, Harry, 46
Hornsby, Rogers, 49, 74, 80, 81, 88, 90, 93, 96, 97, 98, 99, 100, 102, 143
Hubbell, Carl, 101, 105, 106, 109, 111, 112, 113, 115, 116, 117, 118, 120, 121, 122, 123, 124, 125, 126, 127, 129, 131, 134, 136, 138, 139, 141, 144, 149, 151, 215
Huggins, Miller, 49
Hughes, Jim, 195
Hummel, John, 36, 37, 40
Hunter, George, 36

I

Irvin, Monte, 181, 182, 183, 189

J

Jackson, Travis, 82, 93, 95, 97, 104, 108, 111
Jansen, Larry, 165, 169, 171, 172, 174, 175, 176, 178, 181, 182, 183, 189
Johnson, Ban, 16, 52
Johnson, Walter, 88, 89, 210
Johnston, Doc, 74
Johnston, Jimmy, 74, 78, 80, 86
Jones, Oscar, 19, 22
Jones, Randy, 50
Jones, Sheldon, 171, 172, 174, 175
Jonnard, Claud, 84
Jordan, Tim, 26, 28, 29, 33, 34
Jorgensen, Spider, 164
Jurges, Billy, 135

K

Karl, Andy, 155, 158, 159
Kauff, Bernie, 61, 65, 71
Keefe, Tim, 46
Keeler, Wee Willie, 9, 10, 11, 12, 13, 14, 15, 17, 27, 157
Keller, Charlie, 145
Kelley, Joe, 10, 11
Kelly, George, 74, 75, 76, 78, 81, 82, 87, 89, 90, 93, 95
Kennedy, Monte, 162, 163
Kerr, Buddy, 162
Kiner, Ralph, 165, 172, 200, 212
Kitson, Frank, 15, 17
Klein, Chuck, 104, 114
Kluzewski, Ted, 212
Koenecke, Len, 119, 121
Koenig, Mark, 123
Konetchy, Ed, 71
Kopf, Larry, 64
Koslo, Dave, 162, 163, 165, 174, 175, 184, 189
Koufax, Sandy, 199, 202
Koy, Ernie, 133, 136
Kucks, Johnny, 203
Kustus, Joe, 36

L

Labine, Clem, 182, 190, 199, 201, 203
Landis, Kenesaw Mountain, 72
Larsen, Don, 203
Lary, Lyn, 123
Lauder, Billy, 15, 17
Lavagetto, Cookie, 130, 131, 138, 139, 168
Lavender, Jimmy, 56
Layton, Lester, 172
Lazzeri, Tony, 130
Leach, Freddie, 108, 111
Leach, Tommy, 17
Leiber, Hank, 123, 135
Lemon, Bob, 172
Leonard, Dutch, 119, 121
Leslie, Sam, 114, 119, 121, 124, 125, 133
Liddle, Don, 196, 199
Lindstrom, Fred, 97, 101, 103, 105, 108, 111
Lockman, Whitey, 174, 177
Loes, Billy, 184, 185, 195, 199
Lohrman, Bill, 141, 149
Lombardi, Ernie, 114, 140, 151, 153, 158
Lombardi, Vic, 158, 167
Long, Herman, 21
Lopat, Eddie, 182, 185
Lopez, Al, 107, 114, 117
Lumley, Harry, 20, 21, 22, 24, 25, 27, 28, 30, 41
Luque, Dolf, 108, 117
Lush, Johnny, 26

M

Mack, Connie, 16, 42, 209
Maddoz, Nick, 30
Magee, Lee, 72
Maglie, Sal, 160, 176, 181, 182, 183, 186, 189, 194, 196, 199, 201, 203, 204
Maguire, Freddie, 82
Malay, Joe, 123

Mancuso, Gus, 125, 135, 143, 151
Mantle, Mickey, 185
Manush, Heinie, 130, 131
Marberry, Firpo, 84
Maris, Roger, 46, 109
Marquard, Rube, 42, 43, 44, 46, 47, 50, 53, 58, 61, 64, 65, 68
Marshall, Willard, 165, 174, 176, 177
Martin, Billie, 189
Martin, Pepper, 120
Mathewson, Christie, 7, 11, 12, 13, 14, 15, 17, 18, 19, 21, 22, 23, 25, 27, 28, 29, 30, 31, 32, 34, 35, 37, 39, 40, 42, 43, 44, 46, 47, 50, 51, 53, 56, 60, 67, 91, 209, 210, 211, 215
Mathewson, Henry, 28
Matthews, Eddie, 212
Mays, Carl, 73
Mays, Willie, 6, 87, 104, 179, 180, 181, 183, 189, 192, 193, 194, 196, 197, 200, 202, 204, 205, 206, 208, 212, 213
McCarthy, Jack, 41
McCarthy, Joe, 98
McCarthy, Johnny, 129
McCreery, Tom, 17
McDevitt, Danny, 206
McElveen, Humpy, 36
McGann, Dan, 15, 17, 21, 22
McGinnity, Joe (Iron Man), 9, 11, 12, 15, 17, 18, 19, 21, 22, 28
McGraw, John, 7, 15, 16, 17, 18, 21, 23, 24, 27, 29, 32, 33, 42, 43, 45, 47, 50, 52, 53, 60, 63, 64, 71, 73, 76, 80, 81, 84, 86, 87, 89, 90, 91, 93, 94, 96, 97, 98, 99, 101, 102, 105, 107, 111, 113, 171, 209, 211
McIntire, Harry, 25, 26, 28
McKechnie, Bill, 60
McPhail, Larry, 135, 137, 138, 141, 143, 144, 166
McQuillen, Hugh, 86, 89
Medwick, Joe (Ducky), 120, 125, 129, 141, 144, 147, 153, 155, 156

Meer, Johnny Vander, 132, 135, 167, 170
Melton, Cliff, 129, 131, 134, 139, 141, 146, 149, 152
Merkle, Fred, 31, 32, 43, 44, 47, 54, 55, 57, 60
Mertes, Sam, 18, 19, 25
Meusel, Irish, 76, 81, 85, 86, 90, 92, 93
Meyer, Russ, 195, 197
Meyers, Chief, 44, 46, 47, 51, 58
Mitchell, Clarence, 111
Mize, Johnny, 148, 149, 161, 163, 165, 169, 172, 175, 177, 185, 200
Moore, Jo Jo, 114, 120, 125, 129, 130, 135
Morrison, Johnny, 105
Moss, Ray, 105
Mowrey, Harry, 62
Mueller, Don, 189, 190, 193, 200, 202, 206
Mulcahy, Hugh, 145
Mungo, Van Lingle, 111, 114, 115, 117, 118, 119, 121, 123, 124, 127, 131, 144, 158, 159
Murray, Red, 36, 37, 40, 46, 47
Musial, Stan, 150, 157, 171, 188
Myers, Hy, 69, 71, 75, 80

N

Nehf, Art, 74, 75, 78, 81, 89, 97
Newcombe, Don, 173, 175, 177, 178, 179, 180, 181, 182, 184, 199, 200, 201, 203, 204, 205
Newhouser, Hal, 157
Newsom, Bobo, 105, 150
Newton, Doc, 17

O

O'Dea, Ken, 135
O'Doul, Lefty, 102, 110, 112, 114, 115, 120
O'Farrell,Bob, 105
O'Malley, Walter, 192, 193, 206

O'Rourke, Jim, 21
Odwell, Fred, 24
Olmo, Luis, 157, 160
Olson, Ivy, 62
Orengo, Joe, 155
Ott, Mel, 7, 94, 101, 103, 104, 106,
    109, 111, 112, 114, 115, 116,
    118, 120, 121, 123, 124, 125,
    127, 129, 131, 134, 136, 138,
    139, 142, 144, 146, 148, 149,
    151, 152, 153, 155, 156, 158,
    159, 161, 162, 170, 182, 200,
    212, 213, 214
Overall, Orvie, 36, 37
Owen, Mickey, 143, 145, 147, 160,
    168

P

Pafko, Andy, 184
Palica, Erv, 167, 178
Parmalee, Roy, 117, 120, 122, 123
Partridge, Jay, 98
Pastorius, Jim, 26, 30
Perritt, Pol, 60, 61, 63, 67, 69
Petty, Jesse, 95
Pfeffer, Jeff, 54, 55, 57, 59, 61, 65,
    71, 77
Pfiester, Jack, 29
Phelps, Babe, 126, 127, 130
Phelps, Ray, 108
Pipp, Wally, 94
Poat, Ray, 171
Podres, Johnny, 195, 198, 199, 205,
    208
Pressnell, Tot, 133
Pulliam, Harry S., 35

Q

Quinn, Jack, 110

R

Rackley, Marv, 171
Ragan, Pat, 50, 51
Raschi, Vic, 175, 182, 185

Reese, Pee Wee, 6, 141, 143, 146,
    164, 167, 169, 174, 175, 184,
    185, 191, 194, 205
Reiser, Pete, 6, 19, 141, 143, 146,
    147, 149, 160, 163, 166, 169,
    171
Reulbach, Ed, 51
Reuther, Dutch, 80, 85
Reynolds, Allie, 168, 175, 182, 185
Rhodes, Dusty, 196, 202, 207
Rickey, Branch, 5, 90, 150, 154, 166
Rigney, Bill, 202
Ring, Jimmy, 93
Ripple, Jimmy, 129, 131
Roberts, Robin, 177
Robertson, Dave, 60, 61, 63, 65
Robinson, Jackie, 164, 166, 167,
    169, 171, 172, 173, 174, 175,
    178, 181, 182, 184, 186, 188,
    191, 194, 205
Robinson, Wilbert, 7, 47, 52, 56, 57,
    58, 59, 63, 71, 73, 86, 88, 99,
    102, 113
Roe, Preacher, 158, 171, 172, 173,
    175, 178, 179, 181, 182, 184,
    188, 189, 195
Rosen, Goody, 130, 157, 159
Roush, Edd, 96, 105
Rucker, Nap, 30, 34, 36, 37, 39, 40,
    41, 44, 45, 46, 47, 50, 51
Ruppert, Jacob, 83
Ruth, Babe, 6, 13, 44, 49, 54, 60, 61,
    66, 67, 70, 73, 74, 76, 80, 83, 84,
    85, 87, 93, 94, 97, 104, 109, 120,
    122, 158
Ryan, Rosy, 79, 81, 86

S

Sain, Johnny, 170
Sallee, Slim, 69
Scanlan, Doc, 25, 26, 28, 36
Schmidt, Henry, 18, 19
Schmitz, Johnny, 161
Schoendienst, Red, 202
Schultz, Howie, 150

Schumacher, Hal, 117, 120, 121, 122, 124, 126, 129, 135, 141, 142, 144, 146
Schupp, Ferdie, 63, 65
Scott, Jack, 86, 92, 95
Seats, Tom, 158
Selbach, Kip, 11
Selkirk, George, 130
Seminick, Andy, 177
Sentell, Paul, 27
Seymour, Cy, 28, 29, 30
Shafer, Tillie, 51
Shannon, Spike, 30
Shaute, Joe, 110
Sheckard, Jimmy, 12, 13, 14, 17, 19
Sheridan, Jack, 16
Shibe, Ben, 38
Shotton, Burt, 114, 166, 170
Simmons, Al, 120
Simmons, Curt, 177
Sisler, Dick, 177
Smith, Elmer, 74
Smith, Red, 50
Smith, Sherry, 61, 71
Snider, Duke, 7, 171, 174, 175, 178, 181, 184, 185, 187, 188, 190, 191, 194, 197, 199, 200, 202, 204, 205, 206, 208, 212, 213
Snodgrass, Fred, 39, 40, 46
Snyder, Frank, 76
Spahn, Warren, 170
Spooner, Karl, 195
Stallings, George, 53
Stanky, Eddie, 157, 161, 164, 167, 175, 176, 178, 179, 183
Statz, Jigger, 98
Stengel, Casey, 45, 51, 54, 57, 64, 65, 67, 79, 81, 84, 119, 120, 123, 125, 126, 130, 173, 175, 185, 192, 203
Stoneham, Horace, 145, 207
Strang, Sammy, 23, 28
Stricklett, Elmer, 26, 28
Stripp, Joe, 114, 124, 126
Sukeforth, Clyde, 114

T

Tamulis, Vito, 133, 136
Taylor, Charles, 11
Taylor, Danny, 118
Taylor, Dummy, 13, 28
Taylor Harry, 167
Terry, Bill, 90, 97, 101, 104, 106, 107, 108, 109, 111, 112, 113, 115, 116, 118, 120, 121, 123, 124, 125, 129, 145, 214
Tesreau, Jeff, 46, 47, 50, 51, 53, 54, 55, 56, 57, 60, 67
Thompson, Hank, 177, 178, 189, 193
Thomson, Bobby, 174, 175, 177, 178, 179, 180, 181, 182, 184, 186, 189, 190, 193
Thorpe, Jim, 64
Thurston, Sloppy, 114
Tinker, Joe, 28, 32, 49
Tobin, Jim, 154
Toney, Fred, 64, 71, 74, 75
Toporcer, Specs, 78

V

Vance, Dazzy, 7, 80, 81, 85, 86, 87, 89, 91, 92, 95, 100, 102, 103, 105, 107, 108, 109, 110, 112, 114, 123, 210, 211
VanHaltren, George, 13, 14
Vaughan, Arky, 151
Vaughn, Hippo, 64
Voiselle, Bill, 155, 156, 158, 159

W

Waddell, Rube, 10
Wade, Ben, 184
Wagner, Honus, 10, 18, 19, 45, 65
Walker, Bill, 105, 106, 111, 112
Walker, Dixie, 141, 142, 144, 154, 156, 157, 159, 160, 163, 167, 169
Walker, Nap, 33
Wambsganss, Bill, 74

Y

Z